FIX-IT and FORGET-IT®
EVERYDAY
INSTANT POT®
FAVORITES

Fix-It and Forget-It® EVERYDAY INSTANT POT® FAVORITES

100 Dinners, Sides & Desserts

HOPE COMERFORD

Photos by Bonnie Matthews

Good Books

New York, New York

Good Books books may be purchased in bulk at special discounts for sales promotion, corporate gifts, fund-raising, or educational purposes. Special editions can also be created to specifications. For details, contact the Special Sales Department, Good Books, 307 West 36th Street, 11th Floor, New York, NY 10018 or info@skyhorsepublishing.com.

Good Books is an imprint of Skyhorse Publishing, Inc.®, a Delaware corporation.

Visit our website at www.goodbooks.com.

10 9 8 7 6 5 4 3 2 1

Library of Congress Cataloging-in-Publication Data

Names: Comerford, Hope, author. | Matthews, Bonnie.
Title: Fix-it and forget-it everyday instant pot favorites : 100 dinners,
   sides & desserts / Hope Comerford ; photos by Bonnie Matthews.
Description: New York, New York : Good Books, [2023] | Series: Fix-it and
   forget-it | Includes index. | Summary: "100 quick and easy meals to
   simplify your cooking routines!"-- Provided by publisher.
Identifiers: LCCN 2022031114 (print) | LCCN 2022031115 (ebook) | ISBN
   9781680998610 (trade paperback) | ISBN 9781680998764 (epub)
Subjects: LCSH: Smart cookers. | Quick and easy cooking. | One-dish meals.
   | LCGFT: Cookbooks.
Classification: LCC TX840.S63 C65 2023 (print) | LCC TX840.S63 (ebook) |
   DDC 641.5/87--dc23/eng/20220809
LC record available at https://lccn.loc.gov/2022031114
LC ebook record available at https://lccn.loc.gov/2022031115

Cover design by David Ter-Avanesyan
Cover photo by Bonnie Matthews

Print ISBN: 978-1-68099-861-0
Ebook ISBN: 978-1-68099-876-4

Printed in China

Contents

Welcome to Fix-It and Forget-It Everyday Instant Pot Favorites

"What's for dinner?" just got a little bit easier, now that this book is in hand. Welcome to *Fix-It and Forget-It Everyday Instant Pot Favorites*, where you now have access to 100 of our community's favorite dinners, sides, and desserts.

Whether you feel like breakfast for dinner, soup for dinner, or a traditional dinner, you'll have plenty of recipes to choose from. Dishes like Tuscan Chicken, Macaroni and Cheese, Lasagna the Instant Pot Way, Mississippi Pot Roast, and more will fill your bellies with the types of dinners our community craves the most. If you're looking for a change of pace, you could try the Egg Bites or Shredded Potato Omelet for dinner instead.

You may even find yourself purchasing a second (or third) Instant Pot so you can cook your sides and dessert right along with your main course! Get ready to fire up that Instant Pot because your next everyday favorite recipe is just a few pages away.

What Is an Instant Pot?

In short, an Instant Pot is a digital pressure cooker that also has multiple other functions. Not only can it be used as a pressure cooker, but depending on which model Instant Pot you have, you can set it to do things like sauté, as well as cook rice, grains, porridge, soups/stews, beans/chili, meat, poultry, cake, and eggs, and make yogurt. You can use the Instant Pot to steam or slow cook or even set it manually. Because the Instant Pot has so many functions, it takes away the need for multiple appliances on your counter and allows you to use fewer pots and pans.

Getting Started with Your Instant Pot

Get to Know Your Instant Pot . . .

The very first thing most Instant Pot owners do is called the water test. It helps you get to know your Instant Pot a bit, familiarizes you with it, and might even take a bit of your apprehension away (because if you're anything like me, I was scared to death to use it).

Step 1: Plug in your Instant Pot. This may seem obvious to some, but when we're nervous about using a new appliance, sometimes we forget things like this.

Step 2: Make sure the inner pot is inserted in the cooker. You should *never* attempt to cook anything in your device without the inner pot, or you will ruin your Instant Pot. Food should never come into contact with the actual housing unit.

Step 3: The inner pot has lines for each cup. Fill the inner pot with water until it reaches the 3-cup line.

Step 4: Check the sealing ring to be sure it's secure and in place. You should not be able to move it around. If it's not in place properly, you may experience issues with the pot letting out a lot of steam while cooking, or not coming to pressure.

Step 5: Seal the lid. There is an arrow on the lid between and "open" and "close." There is also an arrow on the top of the base of the Instant Pot between a picture of a locked lock and an unlocked lock. Line those arrows up, then turn the lid toward the picture of the lock (left).You will hear a noise that will indicate the lid is locked. If you do not hear a noise, it's not locked. Try it again.

Step 6: *Always* check to see if the steam valve on top of the lid is turned to "sealing." If it's not on "sealing" and is on "venting," it will not be able to come to pressure.

Step 7: Press the "Steam" button and use the +/- arrow to set it to 2 minutes. Once it's at the desired time, you don't need to press anything else. In a few seconds, the Instant Pot will begin all on its own. For those of us with digital slow cookers, we have a tendency to look for the "start" button, but there isn't one on the Instant Pot.

Step 8: Now you wait for the "magic" to happen! The cooking will begin once the device comes to pressure. This can take anywhere from 5 to 30 minutes, in my experience. Then, you will see the countdown happen (from the time you set it for). After that, the Instant Pot will beep, which means your meal is done!

Step 9: Your Instant Pot will now automatically switch to "warm" and begin a count of how many minutes it's been on warm. The next part is where you either wait for the NPR, or natural pressure release (the pressure releases on its own) or do what's called a QR, or quick release (you manually release the pressure). Which method you choose depends on what you're cooking, but in this case, you can choose either, because it's just water. For NPR, you will wait for the lever to move all the way back over to "venting" and watch the pinion (float valve) next to the lever. It will be flush with the lid when at full pressure and will drop when the pressure is done releasing. If you choose QR, be very careful not to have your hands over the vent, as the steam is very hot and you can burn yourself.

The Three Most Important Buttons You Need to Know About

You will find the majority of recipes will use the following three buttons:

Manual/Pressure Cook: Some older models tend to say "Manual," and the newer models seem to say "Pressure Cook." They mean the same thing. From here, you use the +/- button to change the cook time. After several seconds, the Instant Pot will begin its process. The exact name of this button will vary on your model of Instant Pot.

Sauté: Many recipes will have you sauté vegetables, or brown meat before beginning the pressure cooking process. For this setting, you will not use the lid of the Instant Pot.

Keep Warm/Cancel: This may just be the most important button on the Instant Pot. When you forget to use the +/- buttons to change the time for a recipe, or you press a wrong button, you can hit "keep warm/cancel" and it will turn your Instant Pot off for you.

For a list of helpful accessories for your Instant Pot, such as a silicone egg cup, see page 10.

A springform pan is helpful for desserts like the Lemon Pudding Cake (page 203).

What Do All the Buttons Do?

With so many buttons, it's hard to remember what each one does or means. You can use this as a quick guide in a pinch.

Soup/Broth. This button cooks at high pressure for 30 minutes. It can be adjusted using the +/- buttons to cook more, for 40 minutes, or less, for 20 minutes.

Meat/Stew. This button cooks at high pressure for 35 minutes. It can be adjusted using the +/- buttons to cook more, for 45 minutes, or less, for 20 minutes.

Bean/Chili. This button cooks at high pressure for 30 minutes. It can be adjusted using the +/- buttons to cook more, for 40 minutes, or less, for 25 minutes.

Poultry. This button cooks at high pressure for 15 minutes. It can be adjusted using the +/- buttons to cook more, for 30 minutes, or less, for 5 minutes.

Rice. This button cooks at low pressure and is the only fully automatic program. It is for cooking white rice and will automatically adjust the cooking time depending on the amount of water and rice in the cooking pot.

Multigrain. This button cooks at high pressure for 40 minutes. It can be adjusted using the +/- buttons to cook more, for 45 minutes of warm water soaking time and 60 minutes pressure cooking time, or less, for 20 minutes.

Porridge. This button cooks at high pressure for 20 minutes. It can be adjusted using the +/- buttons to cook more, for 30 minutes, or less, for 15 minutes.

Steam. This button cooks at High pressure for 10 minutes. It can be adjusted using the +/- buttons to cook more, for 15 minutes, or less, for 3 minutes. Always use a rack or steamer basket with this function, because it heats at full power continuously while it's coming to pressure, and you do not want food in direct contact with the bottom of the pressure cooking pot or it will burn. Once it reaches pressure, the steam button regulates pressure by cycling on and off, similar to the other pressure buttons.

Less | Normal | More. Adjust between the *Less | Normal | More* settings by pressing the same cooking function button repeatedly until you get to the desired setting. (Older versions use the *Adjust* button.)

+/- *Buttons*. Adjust the cook time up [+] or down [-]. (On newer models, you can also press and hold [-] or [+] for 3 seconds to turn sound OFF or ON.)

Cake. This button cooks at high pressure for 30 minutes. It can be adjusted using the +/- buttons to cook more, for 40 minutes, or less, for 25 minutes.

Egg. This button cooks at high pressure for 5 minutes. It can be adjusted using the +/- buttons to cook more, for 6 minutes, or less, for 4 minutes.

Instant Pot Tips & Tricks and Other Things You May Not Know

- Never attempt to cook directly in the Instant Pot without the inner pot!

- Once you set the time, you can walk away. It will show the time you set it to, then will change to the word "on" while the pressure builds. Once the Instant Pot has come to pressure, you will once again see the time you set it for. It will count down from there.

- Always make sure the sealing ring is securely in place. If it shows signs of wear or tear, it needs to be replaced.

- Have a sealing ring for savory recipes and a separate sealing ring for sweet recipes. Many people report their desserts tasting like a roast (or another savory food) if they try to use the same sealing ring for all recipes.

- The stainless steel rack (trivet) the Instant Pot comes with can used to keep food from being completely submerged in liquid, like baked potatoes or ground beef. It can also be used to set another pot on, for pot-in-pot cooking.

- If you use warm or hot liquid instead of cold liquid, you may need to adjust the cooking time, or the food may not come out done.

- Always double-check to see that the valve on the lid is set to "sealing" and not "venting" when you first lock the lid. This will save you from the Instant Pot not coming to pressure.

- Use Natural Pressure Release for tougher cuts of meat, recipes with high starch (like rice or grains), and recipes with a high volume of liquid. This means you let the Instant Pot naturally release pressure. The little bobbin will fall once pressure is released completely.

- Use Quick Release for more delicate cuts of meat, such as seafood and chicken breasts, and for steaming vegetables. This means you manually turn the vent (being careful not to put your hand over the vent) to release the pressure. The little bobbin will fall once pressure is released completely.

- Make sure there is a clear pathway for the steam to release. The last thing you want is to ruin the bottom of your cupboards with all that steam.

- You *must* use liquid in the Instant Pot. The *minimum* amount of liquid you should have in the inner pot is ½ cup, but most recipes work best with at least 1 cup.

- Do *not* overfill the Instant Pot! It should only be ½ full for rice or beans (food that expands greatly when cooked), or ⅔ of the way full for almost everything else. Do not fill it to the max fill line.

- In this book, the Cook Time *does not* take into account the amount of time it will take the Instant Pot to come to pressure, or the amount of time it will take the Instant Pot to release pressure. Be aware of this when choosing a recipe to make.

- If the Instant Pot is not coming to pressure, it's usually because the sealing ring is not on properly, or the vent is not set to "sealing."
- The more liquid, or the colder the ingredients, the longer it will take for the Instant Pot to come to pressure.
- Always make sure that the Instant Pot is dry before inserting the inner pot, and make sure the inner pot is dry before inserting it into the Instant Pot.
- Use a binder clip to hold the inner pot tight against the outer pot when sautéing and stirring. This will keep the pot from "spinning" in the base.
- Doubling a recipe does not change the cook time, but instead it will take longer to come up to pressure.
- You do not always need to double the liquid when doubling a recipe. Depending on what you're making, more liquid may make the food too watery. Use your best judgment.
- When using the slow cooker function, use the following chart:

Slow Cooker	Instant Pot
Warm	Less or Low
Low	Normal or Medium
High	More or High

Instant Pot Accessories

Most Instant Pots come with a stainless steel trivet. Below, you will find a list of accessories that will be used in this cookbook. Most of these accessories can be purchased in-store or online.

- Trivet and/or steamer basket—stainless steel or silicone
- 7-inch nonstick springform cake pan
- 7-inch round baking pan
- 7-inch Bundt cake pan
- Sling or trivet with handles
- 1½-quart round baking dish
- Silicone egg bite molds

Dinners

BREAKFAST FOR DINNER

Insta Oatmeal

Hope Comerford, Clinton Township, MI

Makes 2 servings
Prep. Time: 2 minutes ⚘ Cooking Time: 3 minutes

1 cup gluten-free rolled oats
1 tsp. cinnamon
1½ Tbsp. maple syrup
Pinch salt
2 cups unsweetened almond milk

1. Place all ingredients in the inner pot of the Instant Pot and give a quick stir.

2. Secure the lid and set the vent to sealing.

3. Press the Manual button and set the cooking time to 3 minutes.

4. When the cooking time is up, manually release the pressure.

5. Remove the lid and stir. If the oatmeal is still too runny for you, let it sit a few minutes uncovered and it will thicken up.

Serving Suggestion:

Top with ¼ cup of your favorite fruits, like banana slices, raspberries, chopped strawberries, or blueberries.

Oatmeal Complete

Barbara Forrester Landis, Lititz, PA

Makes 6 servings
Prep. Time: 5 minutes & Cooking Time: 4 minutes

I cup water
2 cups uncooked steel cut oats
I cup dried cranberries
I cup walnuts
½ tsp. salt
I Tbsp. cinnamon
I cup water
2 cups nonfat milk

1. Place the steaming rack into the inner pot of the Instant pot and pour in the 1 cup of water.

2. In an approximately 7-cup heat-safe baking dish, add all of your ingredients and stir.

3. Place the dish on top of the steaming rack, close the lid, and secure it to a locking position.

4. Be sure the vent is set to sealing, then set the Instant Pot for 4 minutes on Manual.

5. When it is done cooking, allow the pressure to release naturally.

6. Carefully remove the rack and dish from the Instant Pot and serve.

Cinnamon French Toast Casserole

Hope Comerford, Clinton Township, MI

Makes 8 servings

Prep. Time: 10 minutes ✤ *Cooking Time: 20 minutes*

3 eggs

2 cups milk

¼ cup maple syrup

1 tsp. vanilla extract

1 tsp. cinnamon

Pinch salt

16-oz. loaf cinnamon swirl bread, cubed and left out overnight to go stale

Nonstick cooking spray

1 cup water

1. In a medium bowl, whisk together the eggs, milk, maple syrup, vanilla, cinnamon, and salt. Stir in the cubes of cinnamon swirl bread.

2. You will need a 7-inch round pan for this. Spray the inside with nonstick cooking spray, then pour the bread mixture into the pan.

3. Place the trivet in the bottom of the inner pot, then pour in the water.

4. Make a foil sling and insert it onto the trivet. Carefully place the 7-inch pan on top of the foil sling/trivet.

5. Secure the lid to the locked position, then make sure the vent is turned to sealing.

6. Press the Manual button and use the "+/-" button to set the Instant Pot for 20 minutes.

7. When the cook time is over, let the Instant Pot release naturally for 5 minutes, then quick release the rest.

Serving Suggestion:

Serve with whipped cream and fresh fruit on top, with an extra sprinkle of cinnamon.

The Perfect Instant Pot Hard-Boiled Eggs

Colleen Heatwole, Burton, MI

Makes 6–8 servings
Prep. Time: 10 minutes ⚗ *Cooking Time: 5 minutes*

I cup water
6–8 eggs

1. Pour the water into the inner pot. Place the eggs in a steamer basket, trivet, or egg steamer rack.

2. Close the lid and secure to the locking position. Be sure the vent is turned to sealing. Set for 5 minutes on Manual at high pressure. (It takes about 5 minutes for pressure to build and then 5 minutes to cook.)

3. Let pressure naturally release for 5 minutes, then manually release the remaining pressure.

4. Place the hot eggs into cool water to halt the cooking process. You can peel the cooled eggs immediately or refrigerate them unpeeled.

Egg Bites

Hope Comerford, Clinton Township, MI

Makes 14 mini quiches
Prep. Time: 15 minutes & Cooking Time: 11 minutes & Cooling Time: 5 minutes

2 tsp. olive oil

½ green bell pepper, diced

¼ cup finely chopped broccoli florets

½ small onion, diced

5 oz. fresh spinach

Nonstick cooking spray

8 eggs

¼ cup nonfat milk

3 drops hot sauce, *optional*

⅓ cup shredded reduced-fat cheddar cheese

1 cup water

1. In a small pan on the stove, heat the olive oil over medium-high heat. Sauté the bell pepper, broccoli, and onion for about 8 minutes. Add the spinach and continue to cook until wilted.

2. Spray 2 egg molds with nonstick cooking spray. Divide the cooked vegetables evenly between the egg bite mold cups.

3. In a bowl, whisk the eggs, milk, and hot sauce (if using). Divide this evenly between the egg bite mold cups, or until each cup is ⅔ of the way full.

4. Evenly divide the shredded cheese between the cups. Cover them tightly with foil.

5. Pour the water into the inner pot of the Instant Pot. Place the trivet on top, then place the 2 filled egg bite molds on top of the trivet, the top one stacked staggered on top of the one below.

6. Secure the lid and set the vent to sealing.

7. Manually set the cook time for 11 minutes on high pressure.

8. When the cook time is up, let the pressure release naturally for 5 minutes, then manually release the remaining pressure.

9. When the pin drops, remove the lid and carefully lift the trivet and molds out with oven mitts.

10. Place the molds on a wire rack and uncover. Let cool for about 5 minutes, then pop them out onto a plate or serving platter.

Serving Suggestion:
Serve alongside your favorite healthy bread and a bowl of fruit.

Easy Quiche

Becky Bontrager Horst, Goshen, IN

Makes 6 servings, 1 slice per serving
Prep. Time: 15 minutes & Cooking Time: 25 minutes

1 cup water

Nonstick cooking spray

¼ cup chopped onion

¼ cup chopped mushrooms, *optional*

3 oz. shredded reduced-fat cheddar cheese

2 Tbsp. bacon bits, chopped ham, or browned sausage

4 eggs

¼ tsp. salt

1½ cups nonfat milk

½ cup whole wheat flour

1 Tbsp. trans-fat–free soft margarine

1. Pour the water into the inner pot of the Instant Pot and place the steaming rack inside.

2. Spray a 7-inch round baking pan with nonstick cooking spray.

3. Sprinkle the onion, mushrooms, shredded cheddar, and meat in the cake pan.

4. In a medium bowl, combine the remaining ingredients. Pour them over the meat and vegetables.

5. Place the baking pan onto the steaming rack, close the lid, and secure to the locking position. Be sure the vent is turned to sealing. Set for 25 minutes on Manual at high pressure.

6. Let the pressure release naturally.

7. Carefully remove the cake pan with the handles of the steaming rack and allow to stand for 10 minutes before cutting and serving.

Breakfast for Dinner Casserole

Hope Comerford, Clinton Township, MI

Makes 4–6 servings
Prep. Time: 15 minutes ♠ Cooking Time: 25 minutes

1 Tbsp. olive oil

½ lb. bulk breakfast sausage

½ cup finely diced onion

1 cup water

Nonstick cooking spray

½ lb. frozen Tater Tots or hash browns

6 eggs

¼ cup half-and-half

½ tsp. salt

½ tsp. garlic powder

¼ tsp. black pepper

⅛ tsp. cayenne pepper

½ cup diced bell pepper (any color you wish)

1 cup shredded pepper Jack cheese

½ cup shredded cheddar cheese

Variation:

You can use any types of cheese that your family likes. You do not have to stick with what is suggested above. Also, you could use bacon instead of sausage, or omit the meat altogether.

1. Set the Instant Pot to the Sauté function and add the olive oil.

2. Add the bulk sausage and onion to the inner pot of the Instant Pot and cook until browned. Remove it from the Instant Pot and set aside. Press the Cancel button.

3. Carefully wipe out the inside of the Instant Pot. Pour in the water and scrape the bottom, to be sure there is nothing stuck. Place the trivet on top with handles up.

4. Grease a 7-inch baking pan with butter or nonstick cooking spray. Arrange the Tater Tots or hash browns evenly around the bottom of the pan.

5. In a bowl, mix together the eggs, half-and-half, salt, garlic powder, black pepper, and cayenne. Stir in the bell pepper and pepper Jack cheese. Pour this over the hash browns.

6. Sprinkle the cheddar over the top of the casserole. Cover with foil. Carefully lower the baking pan onto the trivet.

7. Secure the lid and set the vent to sealing. Manually set the cook time for 25 minutes on high pressure.

8. When the cook time is over, let the pressure release naturally for 10 minutes, then manually release the remaining pressure.

9. With hot pads, carefully remove the baking pan with the handles of the trivet. Uncover, serve, and enjoy!

Shredded Potato Omelet

Mary H. Nolt, East Earl, PA

Makes 6 servings
Prep. Time: 15 minutes ☙ *Cooking Time: 20 minutes*

Nonstick cooking spray

3 slices bacon, cooked and crumbled

2 cups shredded cooked potatoes

¼ cup minced onion

¼ cup minced green bell pepper

I cup egg substitute

¼ cup nonfat milk

¼ tsp. salt

⅛ tsp. black pepper

I cup 75%-less-fat shredded cheddar cheese

I cup water

1. With nonstick cooking spray, spray the inside of a round baking dish that will fit in your Instant Pot inner pot.

2. Sprinkle the bacon, potatoes, onion, and bell pepper around the bottom of the baking dish.

3. Mix together the egg substitute, milk, salt, and pepper in mixing bowl. Pour over potato mixture.

4. Top with cheese.

5. Add water to the inner pot, place the steaming rack into the bottom of the inner pot and then place the round baking dish on top.

6. Close the lid and secure to the locking position. Be sure the vent is turned to sealing. Set for 20 minutes on Manual at high pressure.

7. Let the pressure release naturally.

8. Carefully remove the baking dish with the handles of the steaming rack and allow to stand for 10 minutes before cutting and serving.

FAVORITE DINNER
SOUPS, STEWS & CHILIES

Super Healthy Cabbage Soup

Hope Comerford, Clinton Township, MI

Makes 8–10 servings
Prep. Time: 10 minutes   Cooking Time: 5 minutes

1 Tbsp. olive oil

1½ cups chopped onion

3 carrots, halved and sliced

2 celery stalks, halved and sliced

3–4 cups vegetable or chicken broth, *divided*

14½-oz. can diced tomatoes

3 cups chopped cabbage

1 jalapeño, seeded and diced

1 Tbsp. garlic powder

3 tsp. salt

1 tsp. basil

1 tsp. oregano

¼ tsp. pepper

46 oz. no-salt-added tomato juice

1. Turn the Instant Pot to the Sauté function and let it get hot. Add the olive oil.

2. Sauté the onions, carrots, and celery for 3–5 minutes. Add 1 cup of the broth and scrape the bottom of the inner pot to get off any stuck-on bits. Press Cancel.

3. Add the remaining ingredients, including the remaining broth. You do not want to fill your pot all the way to the fill line. So, use a bit less broth if needed to not reach fill line.

4. Secure the lid and set the vent to sealing. Manually set the cook time for 5 minutes on high pressure.

5. When cook time is up, let the pressure release naturally for 10 minutes, then manually release the remaining pressure.

Potato Soup

Michele Ruvola, Vestal, NY

Makes 4 servings
Prep. Time: 20 minutes ⚖ *Cooking Time: 5 minutes*

5 lb. russet potatoes, peeled and cubed

3 celery stalks, sliced thin

I large onion, diced

I clove garlic, minced

I Tbsp. seasoning salt

I tsp. ground black pepper

¼ cup butter

I lb. bacon, fried crisp, rough chopped

4 cups chicken stock

I cup heavy cream

½ cup whole milk

Sour cream, shredded cheddar cheese, sliced green onions for garnish, *optional*

1. Put potatoes, celery, onion, garlic, seasoning salt, pepper, and butter in the inner pot of the Instant Pot. Stir to combine.

2. Add bacon and chicken stock, then stir to combine.

3. Secure the lid and make sure the vent is on sealing. Push the Manual mode button, then set timer for 5 minutes on high pressure.

4. Quick release the steam when cook time is up.

5. Remove lid; mash potatoes to make a semismooth soup.

6. Add cream and milk; stir to combine.

7. Serve with garnishes if desired.

Serving Suggestion:
Perfect on a cold night with slices of bread on the side or a salad.

Mediterranean Lentil Soup

Marcia S. Myer, Manheim, PA

Makes 6 servings
Prep. Time: 10 minutes & Cooking Time: 18 minutes

2 Tbsp. olive oil

2 large onions, chopped

1 carrot, chopped

1 cup uncooked lentils

½ tsp. dried thyme

½ tsp. dried marjoram

3 cups low-sodium chicken stock or vegetable stock

14½-oz. can diced no-salt-added tomatoes

¼ cup chopped fresh parsley

¼ cup sherry, *optional*

⅔ cup grated low-fat cheese, *optional*

1. Set the Instant Pot to the Sauté function, then heat up the olive oil.

2. Sauté the onions and carrot until the onions are translucent, about 5 minutes.

3. Press the Cancel button, then add the lentils, thyme, marjoram, chicken stock, and canned tomatoes.

4. Secure the lid and set the vent to sealing.

5. Manually set the cook time to 18 minutes at high pressure.

6. When the cooking time is over, manually release the pressure.

7. When the pin drops, stir in the parsley and sherry (if using).

8. When serving, add a sprinkle of grated low-fat cheese if you wish.

Veggie Minestrone

Dorothy VanDeest, Memphis, TN

Makes 8 servings
Prep. Time: 5 minutes ⚬ *Cooking Time: 4 minutes*

2 Tbsp. olive oil

1 large onion, chopped

1 clove garlic, minced

4 cups low-sodium chicken, or vegetable stock

16-oz. can kidney beans, rinsed and drained

14½-oz. can no-salt-added diced tomatoes

2 medium carrots, sliced thin

¼ tsp. dried oregano

¼ tsp. pepper

½ cup whole wheat elbow macaroni, uncooked

4 oz. fresh spinach

½ cup grated Parmesan cheese

1. Set the Instant Pot to the Sauté function and heat the olive oil.

2. When the olive oil is heated, add the onion and garlic to the inner pot and sauté for 5 minutes.

3. Press Cancel and add the stock, kidney beans, tomatoes, carrots, oregano, and pepper. Gently pour in the macaroni, but *do not stir.* Just push the noodles gently under the liquid.

4. Secure the lid and set the vent to sealing.

5. Manually set the cook time for 4 minutes on high pressure.

6. When the cooking time is over, manually release the pressure and remove the lid when the pin drops.

7. Stir in the spinach and let wilt a few minutes.

8. Sprinkle 1 Tbsp. grated Parmesan on each individual bowl of this soup. Enjoy!

Cannellini Bean Soup

Hope Comerford, Clinton Township, MI

Makes 6–8 servings
Prep. Time: 10 minutes ⚶ Soaking Time: overnight ⚶ Cooking Time: 30 minutes

2 Tbsp. extra-virgin olive oil

4 cloves garlic, sliced very thin

1 small onion, chopped

2 heads escarole, well washed and cut medium-fine (about 8 cups)

8-oz. bag dry cannellini beans, soaked overnight

8 cups low-sodium chicken stock

3 basil leaves, chopped fine

Parmesan cheese shavings, *optional*

1. Set the Instant Pot to Sauté and heat the olive oil.

2. Sauté the garlic, onion, and escarole until the onion is translucent.

3. Hit the Cancel button on your Instant Pot and add the beans and chicken stock.

4. Secure the lid and set the vent to sealing.

5. Manually set the time for 25 minutes on high pressure.

6. When the cooking time is over, let the pressure release naturally. Remove the lid when the pin drops and spoon into serving bowls.

7. Top each bowl with a sprinkle of the chopped basil leaves and a few Parmesan shavings (if using).

Tip:

If you do not remember to soak the beans overnight, or if you don't have time to soak them, simply cook the soup on high pressure for 51 minutes instead.

Black Bean Soup

Colleen Heatwole, Burton, MI

Makes 4–6 servings
Prep. Time: 10 minutes ⚬ *Cooking Time: 40 minutes*

2 cups dry black beans, cleaned of debris and rinsed

I cup coarsely chopped onion

3 cloves garlic, minced

½ tsp. paprika

⅛ tsp. red pepper flakes

2 large bay leaves

I tsp. cumin

2 tsp. oregano

½ tsp. salt (more if desired)

6 cups vegetable or chicken broth

Yogurt or sour cream, for garnish, *optional*

Shredded cheese, for garnish, *optional*

Diced bell pepper, for garnish, *optional*

1. Place all ingredients, except the yogurt or sour cream, into the inner pot of the Instant Pot.

2. Secure the lid and set the vent to sealing. Manually set the cook time for 40 minutes on high pressure.

3. When cook time is up, let pressure release naturally for 10 minutes, then manually release the remaining pressure.

4. Open the lid. Remove the bay leaves and discard them. Serve with desired garnishes.

Split Pea Soup

Judy Gascho, Woodburn, OR

Makes 3–4 servings
Prep. Time: 20 minutes   Cooking Time: 15 minutes

4 cups chicken broth

4 sprigs thyme

4 oz. ham, diced (about ⅓ cup)

2 Tbsp. butter

2 celery stalks

2 carrots

1 large leek

3 cloves garlic

1½ cups dried green split peas (about 12 oz.)

Salt and pepper to taste

1. Pour the broth into the inner pot of the Instant Pot and set to Sauté. Add the thyme, ham, and butter.

2. While the broth heats, chop the celery and cut the carrots into ½-inch-thick rounds. Halve the leek lengthwise and thinly slice. Chop the garlic. Add the vegetables to the pot as you cut them. Rinse the split peas in a colander, discarding any small stones, then add to the pot.

3. Secure the lid, making sure the steam valve is in the sealing position. Set the cooker to Manual at high pressure for 15 minutes. When the time is up, carefully turn the steam valve to the venting position to release the pressure manually.

4. Turn off the Instant Pot. Remove the lid and stir the soup; discard the thyme sprigs.

5. Thin the soup with up to 1 cup water if needed (the soup will continue to thicken as it cools). Season with salt and pepper.

Three-Bean Chili

Chris Kaczynski, Schenectady, NY

Makes 6 servings
Prep. Time: 10 minutes & Cooking Time: 5 minutes

1 medium onion, diced

16-oz. can low-sodium red kidney beans, drained

16-oz. can low-sodium black beans, drained

16-oz. can low-sodium white kidney or garbanzo beans, drained

14-oz. can low-sodium crushed tomatoes

14-oz. can low-sodium diced tomatoes

1 cup medium salsa

1¼-oz. pkg. dry chili seasoning

1 Tbsp. sugar

1 cup vegetable stock

Shredded cheese and sliced jalapeños, for garnish, *optional*

1. Place all ingredients into the inner pot of the Instant Pot.

2. Secure the lid and set the vent to sealing. Manually set the cook time for 5 minutes on high pressure.

3. When cook time is up, let the pressure release naturally for 10 minutes, then manually release the remaining pressure. Add toppings or garnishes as desired.

Family Favorite Chicken Fajita Soup

Maria Shevlin, Sicklerville, NJ

Makes 10–12 servings
Prep. Time: 20 minutes   ♣   Cooking Time: 5 minutes

1 Tbsp. olive oil

1 medium onion, chopped

5 celery stalks, sliced down the center lengthwise, then chopped

4 cloves garlic, minced

1 cup frozen corn

5 cups chicken stock

2 cups water

32 oz. picante sauce (we love Pace)

¾ tsp. cumin

1 heaping Tbsp. chili powder

1 heaping Tbsp. paprika

½ cup celery leaves, chopped

4 cups precooked chicken (you can use a rotisserie chicken for this)

15-oz. can black beans, rinsed and drained

3 bell peppers, chopped

Optional toppings:

Green onion, chopped

Tortilla strips

Sour cream

Mexican blend or taco-flavored shredded cheese

Sliced jalapeños

1. Set the Instant Pot to the Sauté setting and let it get hot. Add the oil.

2. Sauté the onion, celery, and garlic for approximately 3–5 minutes.

3. Add the corn and mix well

4. Stir in the chicken stock, water, picante sauce, and spices, including the celery leaves.

5. Add the precooked chicken, beans, and peppers, and mix well.

6. Secure the lid and set the vent to sealing. Manually set the cook time for 5 minutes on high pressure.

7. When cook time is up, manually release the pressure.

8. To serve, ladle into bowls and top with any, or all, of the optional toppings you want.

Chicken Stew

Hope Comerford, Clinton Township, MI

Makes 6 servings
Prep. Time: 10 minutes ⚬ Cooking Time: 20 minutes

1 Tbsp. olive oil

1 cup chopped onion

3 carrots, chopped

2 celery stalks, chopped

4 cups chicken broth, *divided*

2 lb. boneless, skinless chicken breasts, diced

4–5 red potatoes, chopped

2½ tsp. salt

3 tsp. garlic powder

3 tsp. onion powder

1½ tsp. Italian seasoning

¼ tsp. pepper

2 bay leaves

2 Tbsp. cornstarch

2 Tbsp. cold water

1. Press Sauté on the Instant Pot. Let it get hot. Add the oil.

2. Sauté the onion, carrots, and celery for about 3–5 minutes.

3. Pour in 1 cup of the broth and scrape the bottom of the inner pot to bring up any stuck-on bits. Press Cancel.

4. Add the chicken, red potatoes, salt, garlic powder, onion powder, Italian seasoning, pepper, bay leaves, and remaining 3 cups of broth.

5. Secure the lid and set the vent to sealing. Manually set the cook time for 10 minutes on high pressure.

6. When cook time is up, let the pressure release naturally for 10 minutes, then manually release the remaining pressure. When the pin drops, remove the lid. Press Cancel.

7. Press the Sauté function once again. Mix the cornstarch and cold water, then stir it into the stew. Let it simmer for about 5 minutes, or until it is thickened. Remove the bay leaves before serving.

Tip:

My family loves stew with crusty Italian or French bread with butter on top.

White Chicken Chili

Hope Comerford, Clinton Township, MI

Makes 4–6 servings
Prep. Time: 5 minutes ⚬ Cooking Time: 14 minutes

2 cans great northern beans, undrained

1 large sweet onion, chopped

16-oz. jar of your favorite salsa

1 Tbsp. cumin

1 tsp. sea salt

¼ tsp. pepper

2 cups chicken stock

2 lb. boneless, skinless chicken breasts

8 oz. shredded pepper Jack cheese

8 oz. shredded Monterey Jack cheese

1. Place the beans, chopped onion, salsa, cumin, salt, pepper, and chicken stock into the inner pot of the Instant Pot, then place the chicken on top.

2. Secure the lid and set the vent to sealing. Manually set the cook time for 14 minutes on high pressure.

3. When cook time is up, manually release the pressure. When the pin drops, remove the lid.

4. Remove the chicken breasts and shred the meat between two forks. Stir it back through the contents of the inner pot, along with the shredded pepper Jack and Monterey Jack cheeses.

Serving suggestion:

This is very good with slices of avocado and crushed tortilla chips on top.

Beef Mushroom Barley Soup

Becky Frey, Lebanon, PA

Makes 8 servings
Prep. Time: 20 minutes & Cooking Time: 25 minutes

2 Tbsp. olive oil, divided
1 lb. boneless beef chuck, cubed
1 large onion, chopped
2 cloves garlic, crushed
1 lb. fresh mushrooms, sliced
1 celery stalk, sliced
2 carrots, sliced
½ tsp. dried thyme, *optional*
8 cups low-sodium beef stock
½ cup uncooked pearl barley
½ tsp. freshly ground pepper
3 Tbsp. chopped fresh parsley

1. Set the Instant Pot to the Sauté function and heat up 1 tablespoon of the olive oil in the inner pot.

2. Brown the beef, in batches if needed, and then remove and set aside.

3. Add the remaining tablespoon of olive oil and sauté the onion, garlic, and mushrooms for 3–4 minutes.

4. Add the beef back in, as well as all the remaining ingredients, except for the parsley. Press Cancel.

5. Secure the lid and set the vent to sealing.

6. Manually set the cook time to 25 minutes on high pressure.

7. When the cooking time is over, let the pressure release naturally for 15 minutes, then manually release the remaining pressure.

8. When the pin drops, remove the lid, and stir. Serve each bowl topped with some fresh chopped parsley.

Chili Comerford Style

Hope Comerford, Clinton Township, MI

Makes 4–6 servings
Prep. Time:10 minutes 🍴 Cooking Time: 15 minutes

1 tsp. olive oil

1 lb. ground round

1 medium onion, chopped

15½-oz. can kidney beans, drained and rinsed

2 (14½-oz.) cans diced tomatoes

10-oz. can cream of tomato soup (I use Pacific Creamy Tomato)

3 cloves garlic, minced

2 tsp. tarragon

1 tsp. salt

1 tsp. pepper

2 tsp. chili powder

1 cup beef stock

3–6 cups water, depending on how thick or thin you like your chili

1. Set the Instant Pot to the Sauté function and let it get hot. Pour in the olive oil and coat the bottom of the pot.

2. Brown the ground round with the onion. This will take about 5–7 minutes.

3. Press Cancel. Carefully drain the grease.

4. Place the remaining ingredients into the inner pot with the beef and onion.

5. Secure the lid and set the vent to sealing. Manually set the cook time for 15 minutes on high pressure.

6. When cook time is up, manually release the pressure. When the pin drops, remove the lid and serve.

Serving suggestion:
We love to add a dollop of sour cream and a bit of shredded sharp cheddar to our chili. Sliced jalapeños make a nice garnish.

Instantly Good Beef Stew

Hope Comerford, Clinton Township, MI

Makes 6 servings
Prep. Time: 20 minutes & Cooking Time: 35 minutes

3 Tbsp. olive oil, *divided*

2 lb. stewing beef, cubed

2 cloves garlic, minced

1 large onion, chopped

3 celery stalks, sliced

3 large potatoes, cubed

2–3 carrots, sliced

8 oz. no-salt-added tomato sauce

10 oz. low-sodium beef broth

2 tsp. Worcestershire sauce

¼ tsp. pepper

1 bay leaf

1. Set the Instant Pot to the Sauté function, then add 1 tablespoon of the oil. Add ⅓ of the beef cubes and brown and sear all sides. Repeat this process twice more with the remaining oil and beef cubes. Set the beef aside.

2. Place the garlic, onion, and celery into the pot and sauté for a few minutes. Press Cancel.

3. Add the beef back in as well as all of the remaining ingredients.

4. Secure the lid and make sure the vent is set to sealing. Choose Manual for 35 minutes.

5. When cook time is up, let the pressure release naturally for 15 minutes, then release any remaining pressure manually.

6. Remove the lid, remove the bay leaf, then serve.

Note:

If you want your stew to be a bit thicker, remove some of the potatoes, mash, then stir them back through the stew.

Ham and Bean Soup

Susie Nisley Millersburg, OH

Makes 10 servings
Prep. Time: 10 minutes ⚭ Cooking Time: 30 minutes

1 lb. extra-lean ham, diced
1 lb. dry navy beans, rinsed
1 small onion, chopped
1 stalk celery, diced
½ carrot, diced
1 cup tomato juice
2 tsp. garlic powder
½ tsp. cumin
½ tsp. black pepper
1 tsp. no-salt seasoning
7 cups reduced sodium chicken stock
1 bunch fresh cilantro, chopped

1. Place all ingredients, except the cilantro, into the inner pot of your Instant Pot.

2. Secure the lid and set the vent to sealing. Manually set the cook time for 30 minutes on high pressure.

3. When cook time is up, let the pressure release naturally.

4. Before serving, stir in the chopped fresh cilantro.

FAVORITE DINNERS

Macaroni and Cheese

Hope Comerford, Clinton Township, MI

Makes 8 servings
Prep. Time: 5 minutes 🍳 Cooking Time: 4 minutes

1 lb. uncooked elbow macaroni

2 cups water

2 cups chicken broth

4 Tbsp. butter

1 tsp. salt

½ tsp. pepper

1 tsp. hot sauce

1 tsp. mustard powder

½–1 cup heavy cream or milk

1 cup shredded Gouda

1 cup shredded sharp cheddar cheese

1 cup shredded Monterey Jack cheese

1. Place the macaroni, water, broth, butter, salt, pepper, hot sauce, and mustard powder into the inner pot of the Instant Pot.

2. Secure the lid and set the vent to sealing. Manually set the cook time for 4 minutes.

3. When the cook time is over, manually release the pressure.

4. When the pin drops, remove the lid and stir in the cream, starting with ½ cup. Begin stirring in the shredded cheese, 1 cup at a time. If the sauce ends up being too thin, let it sit a while and it will thicken up.

Variation:

If you want the mac and cheese to have a crust on top, pour the mac and cheese from the Instant Pot into an oven-safe baking dish. Top with additional cheese and bake in a 325°F oven for about 15 minutes.

Serving suggestion:

Serve with Southwestern Cauliflower (page 195).

Meatless Ziti

Hope Comerford, Clinton Township, MI

Makes 8 servings
Prep. Time: 10 minutes ⚮ Cooking Time: 3 minutes

1 Tbsp. olive oil
1 small onion, chopped
3 cups water, *divided*
15-oz. can crushed tomatoes
8-oz. can tomato sauce
1½ tsp. Italian seasoning
1 tsp. garlic powder
1 tsp. onion powder
1 tsp. sea salt
¼ tsp. pepper
12 oz. ziti
1–2 cups shredded mozzarella cheese

1. Set the Instant Pot to the Sauté function and heat the olive oil.

2. When the oil is hot, sauté the onion for 3 to 5 minutes, or until translucent.

3. Pour in 1 cup of the water and scrape any bits from the bottom of the inner pot with a wooden spoon or spatula.

4. In a bowl, mix together the crushed tomatoes, tomato sauce, Italian seasoning, garlic powder, onion powder, sea salt, and pepper. Pour 1 cup of this in the inner pot and stir.

5. Pour in the ziti. Press it down so it's in there evenly, but do not stir.

6. Pour the remaining pasta sauce evenly over the top. Again, do not stir.

7. Secure the lid and set the vent to sealing. Manually set the cook time for 3 minutes.

8. When the cook time is over, let the pressure release naturally for 10 minutes, then manually release the remaining pressure.

9. When the pin drops, remove the lid and stir in the shredded mozzarella. This will thicken as it sits a bit.

Twisted Shrimp Scampi à la Mamma Ree

Maria Shevlin, Sicklerville, NJ

Makes 4–6 servings
Prep. Time: 30 minutes ⚭ Cooking Time: 20 minutes

2 Tbsp. butter

1 Tbsp. olive oil

3 Tbsp. finely chopped garlic

1 vegetable bouillon cube, dissolved in 1 cup hot water

¼ cup white wine, or broth

2 tsp. Italian seasoning

1 tsp. garlic powder

½ tsp. black pepper

Pinch to 1 tsp. red pepper flakes, *optional* (you may use much less if you prefer as well)

1 medium onion, cut into thin strips

2 red bell peppers, cut into thin strips

1–1½ lb. large shrimp

Cornstarch for dredging

1. Set the Instant Pot to the Sauté function and let it get hot. Add the butter, oil, and chopped garlic to the bottom of the inner pot and sauté for approximately 1 minute, or until butter melts.

2. Add the bouillon and water mixture, wine, and all seasonings.

3. Once brought to a nice simmer, add the onion and bell pepper strips.

4. Simmer, approximately 10 minutes.

5. Meanwhile peel and devein the shrimp and ever so lightly, dredge the shrimp in cornstarch. Shake to remove excess.

6. Add the shrimp directly to the simmering Instant Pot, and push gently into the liquid and veggies.

7. Cook for 3–4 minutes.

8. Stir and simmer for another 3–5 minutes.

Serving suggestions:
Serve over rice, spaghetti, or fettuccine style pasta.

Garlic Galore Rotisserie Chicken

Hope Comerford, Clinton Township, MI

Makes 4 Servings
Prep. Time: 5 minutes ⚭ Cooking Time: 33 minutes

3-lb. whole chicken

2 Tbsp. olive oil, *divided*

Salt to taste

Pepper to taste

20–30 cloves fresh garlic, peeled and left whole

1 cup chicken stock, broth, or water

2 Tbsp. garlic powder

2 tsp. onion powder

½ tsp. basil

½ tsp. cumin

½ tsp. chili powder

Serving suggestion:
Serve with Garlic Butter Cauliflower (page 193) and Mashed Potatoes (page 161).

1. Rub chicken with 1 tablespoon of the olive oil and sprinkle with salt and pepper.

2. Place the garlic cloves inside the chicken. Use butcher's twine to secure the legs.

3. Press the Sauté button on the Instant Pot then add the rest of the olive oil to the inner pot.

4. When the pot is hot, place the chicken inside. You are just trying to sear it, so leave it for about 4 minutes on each side.

5. Remove the chicken and set aside. Place the trivet at the bottom of the inner pot and pour in the chicken stock.

6. Mix together the remaining seasonings and rub the mixture all over the entire chicken.

7. Place the chicken back inside the inner pot, breast side up, on top of the trivet and secure the lid to the sealing position.

8. Press the Manual button and use the +/- to set it for 25 minutes.

9. When the timer beeps, allow the pressure to release naturally for 15 minutes. If the lid will not open at this point, quick release the remaining pressure and remove the chicken.

10. Let the chicken rest for 5–10 minutes before serving.

Butter Chicken

Jessica Stoner, Arlington, OH

Makes 4 servings
Prep. Time: 10–15 minutes   *Cooking Time: 20 minutes*

1 Tbsp. olive oil

1 medium onion, diced

1–2 medium cloves garlic, minced

½ Tbsp. minced ginger

1 tsp. garam masala

½ tsp. turmeric

2 tsp. kosher salt

2 lb. cubed boneless, skinless chicken breasts

¼ cup tomato paste

2 cups crushed tomatoes

1½ cups water

½ Tbsp. honey

1½ cups heavy cream

1 Tbsp. butter

1. On Sauté function at high heat, heat the oil in the inner pot of the Instant Pot. Add the onion, garlic, and ginger and sauté for 1 minute, until fragrant and onion is soft.

2. Add the garam masala, turmeric, and salt. Sauté quickly and add the chicken. Stir to coat chicken. Add the tomato paste and crushed tomatoes. Slowly add the water, scraping the bottom of the pot with a spoon to make sure there are no bits of tomato stuck to the bottom. Stir in the honey.

3. Secure the lid, making sure vent is turned to sealing function. Use the Poultry high pressure function and set cook time to 15 minutes. Once done cooking, do a quick release of the pressure.

4. Remove lid and change to medium/normal Sauté function and stir in the heavy cream and bring to a simmer. Simmer for 5 minutes, adding up to ¼ cup additional water if you need to thin the sauce out. Stir in the butter until melted and turn off.

Serving suggestion:
Serve hot with basmati rice and naan.

Tuscan Chicken

Hope Comerford, Clinton Township, MI

Makes 4 servings
Prep. Time: 5 minutes & Cooking Time: 10 minutes

½ tsp. salt

½ tsp. onion powder

½ tsp. Italian seasoning

¼ tsp. pepper

2 lb. boneless, skinless chicken thighs

3 Tbsp. butter

6 cloves garlic, minced

¾ cup sliced baby bella mushrooms

¾ cup chicken stock

½ tsp. red pepper flakes

1 cup heavy cream

2 cups spinach

½ cup sliced sun-dried tomatoes

½ cup shredded Asiago cheese

Serving suggestion:
Serve over your favorite pasta or Perfect White Rice (page 141).

1. Coat the chicken with the salt, onion powder, Italian seasoning, and pepper.

2. Set the Instant Pot to the Sauté function and let it get hot. Add the butter to melt.

3. When the butter is melted, immediately add the chicken to the inner pot to sear.

4. Once the chicken is seared on both sides, add the garlic and mushrooms. Sauté for about 1 minute.

5. Pour in the chicken stock and carefully deglaze the bottom of the pot, scraping up any stuck-on bits. Press Cancel.

6. Sprinkle in the red pepper flakes, then secure the lid and set the vent to sealing.

7. Manually set the cook time for 5 minutes on high pressure.

8. When cook time is up, manually release the pressure.

9. When the pin drops, remove the lid. Press Cancel, then Sauté. Remove the chicken and set aside.

10. Stir in the heavy cream slowly, then add the spinach, sun-dried tomatoes, and cheese. Once mixed, serve the chicken with the sauce over the top.

Italian Chicken and Broccoli

Liz Clapper, Lancaster, PA

Makes 6 servings
Prep. Time: 15 minutes ⚮ *Cooking Time: 5 minutes*

1 tsp. olive oil

1 head broccoli, chopped into florets (about 4 cups)

2 cloves garlic, finely chopped

1 lb. chicken tenderloins

4 medium carrots, sliced thin

2 cups uncooked whole-grain macaroni pasta

3 cups low-fat, low-sodium chicken broth

1 ½ Tbsp. Italian seasoning

¼ cup shredded reduced-fat Parmesan cheese

1. Set the Instant Pot to Sauté and heat the oil.

2. Sauté the broccoli for 5 minutes in the inner pot. Set it aside in a bowl and cover to keep warm.

3. Add the garlic and chicken and sauté for 8 minutes.

4. Press Cancel. Add the carrots and stir. Pour the macaroni evenly over the top. Pour in the broth and Italian seasoning. Do not stir.

5. Secure the lid and set the vent to sealing.

6. Manually set the cook time for 5 minutes on high pressure.

7. When the cooking time is over, let the pressure release naturally for 5 minutes, then manually release the remaining pressure.

8. When the pin drops, remove the lid, sprinkle the contents with Parmesan, and serve immediately.

Serving suggestion:

Serve with Baked Potatoes (page 157).

Wild 'N Tangy BBQ Chicken

Maria Shevlin, Sicklerville, NJ

Makes 4–6 servings
Prep. Time: 15 minutes ⚬ Cooking Time: 15 minutes

1–2 lb. boneless, skinless chicken thighs

1–2 lb. boneless, skinless chicken breasts

1 cup chicken broth

1 tsp. onion powder

1 tsp. garlic powder

½–1 tsp. chili powder

¼–½ tsp. red pepper flakes

½ tsp. smoked paprika

¼ cup brown sugar

½ cup onion, minced

1½ tsp. parsley flakes

2 cloves garlic, minced

18-oz. bottle of your favorite BBQ sauce

1. Place all the ingredients, except the BBQ sauce, into the inner pot of the Instant Pot.

2. Secure the lid and set the vent to sealing. Manually set the cook time for 15 minutes on high pressure.

3. When cook time is up, let the pressure release naturally for 10 minutes, then manually release the remaining pressure.

4. When the pin drops, remove the lid. Carefully drain most of the broth out and reserve it.

5. Shred the chicken in the pot with your hand mixer or between 2 forks. Note: The hand mixer works like a charm!

6. Add the BBQ sauce and mix well.

7. Taste and adjust seasonings if needed. If it's too dry for your liking, add some of the reserved liquid.

Serving suggestion:

Either serve on a plate, or on slider buns with a side of coleslaw and pickles. You can also try serving it open-faced on Texas toast.

Easy Enchilada Shredded Chicken

Hope Comerford, Clinton Township, MI

Makes 10–14 servings
Prep. Time: 10 minutes & Cooking Time: 10 minutes

5 lb. boneless, skinless chicken thighs, cut into 1½-inch pieces

14½-oz. can petite diced tomatoes

1 medium onion, chopped

8 oz. red enchilada sauce

½ tsp. salt

½ tsp. chili powder

½ tsp. basil

½ tsp. garlic powder

¼ tsp. pepper

1 cup chicken stock

Plain yogurt for garnish, *optional*

Fresh cilantro for garnish, *optional*

1. Place all the ingredients, except the garnishes, into the inner pot of the Instant Pot.

2. Secure the lid and set the vent to sealing. Manually set the cook time for 10 minutes on high pressure.

3. When cook time is up, let the pressure release naturally for 10 minutes, then manually release the remaining pressure.

4. Remove the lid. Take the chicken pieces out, shred the chicken between two forks, and mix the chicken back into the juices in the pot.

5. Serve with the yogurt and cilantro if desired.

Serving suggestions:

Serve over salad, brown rice, quinoa, sweet potatoes, nachos, or soft-shell corn tortillas. Goes well with Hometown Spanish Rice (page 151) as well.

Salsa Lime Chicken

Maria Shevlin, Sicklerville, NJ

Makes 2–4 servings
Prep. Time: 10 minutes & Cooking Time: 17 minutes

4 bone-in, skin-on chicken thighs

1 tsp. chili lime seasoning

½ tsp. True Lime Garlic Cilantro Spice Blend

2 tsp. olive oil

1 cup diced onion

1 cup chicken broth

1½ cups of your favorite salsa

1 lime, zested and juiced

2 tsp. garlic powder

2 pkg. True Lime Crystallized Lime Packets

¼ cup brown sugar

1. Season both sides of chicken with chili lime seasoning, and cilantro lime seasoning.

2. Set the Instant Pot to Sauté and let it get hot.

3. Add the olive oil to the inner pot, then sauté the chicken, skin-side down, for 3–4 minutes.

4. Turn the chicken over to brown on other side.

5. Add the onion, broth, salsa, lime juice and zest, garlic powder, lime crystals, and brown sugar. Scrape the bottom of the pot and give it a quick stir.

6. Secure the lid and set the vent to sealing. Manually set the cook time for 9 minutes on high pressure.

7. When cook time is up, manually release the pressure.

Serving suggestions:
Serve with green beans and warm tortillas.

Sweet-and-Sour Chicken

Maria Shevlin, Sicklerville, NJ

Makes 3–4 servings
Prep. Time: 15–30 minutes ☙ *Cooking Time: 15 minutes*

1 Tbsp. olive oil

1 lb. boneless, skinless chicken breasts, cubed

¼ cup water chestnuts

¼ tsp. salt

½ tsp. paprika

½ tsp. ground ginger

¼ tsp. black pepper

1 medium onion, cubed

2 cups bell peppers, any color, cubed

Sauce:

2 Tbsp. ketchup

½ cup white vinegar

½ cup sweetener of your choice

1 Tbsp. coconut aminos or soy sauce

1 tsp. garlic powder

½ tsp. pineapple extract

½ cup chicken stock

1. Set the Instant Pot to the Sauté setting and let it get hot. Add the oil.

2. Add the chicken to the inner pot and brown it lightly. Press Cancel.

3. Add the water chestnuts, salt, paprika, ginger, and pepper.

4. Add the onions, peppers, and all ingredients for sauce.

5. Secure the lid and set the vent to sealing. Manually set the cook time for 10 minutes.

6. When cook time is up, release the pressure manually.

Serving suggestions:

Enjoy with ramen-style noodles or basmati rice with green onions on top.

Hawaiian Chicken Tacos

Maria Shevlin, Sicklerville, NJ

Makes 8–10 servings
Prep. Time: 15 minutes ⚭ Cooking Time: 15 minutes

6 boneless, skinless chicken thighs

20-oz. can crushed pineapple and its juice

½ cup brown sugar

2 (10¾-oz.) cans tomato soup

1 bunch green onions, chopped

Tortillas or hard taco shells, for serving

Optional Garnishes:

Sesame seeds

Shredded lettuce

Red onion

Green onion

1. Add chicken thighs to the bottom of Instant Pot inner pot and add all remaining ingredients on top.

2. Secure the lid and set the vent to sealing. Cook on the Poultry setting for 15 minutes.

3. When cook time is up, let the pressure release naturally for 5 minutes, and then manually release the remaining pressure.

4. When the pin drops, remove the lid. Shred the chicken by using 2 forks directly in the Instant Pot.

5. Add to tortillas or hard taco shells and add any or all the garnishments listed above.

Serving suggestion:

Serve with pineapple fried rice if desired.

Mild Chicken Curry with Coconut Milk

Brittney Horst, Lititz, PA

Makes 4–6 servings
Prep. Time: 10 minutes ❦ *Cooking Time: 14 minutes*

1 large onion, diced

6 cloves garlic, crushed

¼ cup coconut oil

½ tsp. black pepper

½ tsp. turmeric

½ tsp. paprika

¼ tsp. cinnamon

¼ tsp. cloves

¼ tsp. cumin

¼ tsp. ginger

½ tsp. salt

1 Tbsp. curry powder (more if you like more flavor)

½ tsp. chili powder

24-oz. can of low-sodium diced or crushed tomatoes

13½-oz. can of light coconut milk (I prefer a brand that has no unwanted ingredients, like guar gum or sugar)

4 lb. boneless, skinless chicken breasts, cut into chunks

1. Sauté onion and garlic in the coconut oil, either with Sauté setting in the inner pot of the Instant Pot or on stove top, then add to pot.

2. Combine spices in a small bowl, then add to the inner pot.

3. Add tomatoes and coconut milk and stir.

4. Add chicken and stir to coat the pieces with the sauce.

5. Secure the lid and make sure vent is at sealing. Set to Manual mode (or Pressure Cook on newer models) for 14 minutes.

6. Let pressure release naturally (if you're crunched for time, you can do a quick release).

7. Serve with your favorite sides and enjoy!

Serving suggestion:
We like it on rice, with a couple of veggies on the side.

Insta Pasta à la Maria

Maria Shevlin, Sicklerville, NJ

Makes 6–8 servings
Prep. Time: 10–15 minutes ⚶ Cooking Time: 6 minutes

32-oz. jar of your favorite spaghetti sauce or 1 qt. of homemade

2 cups fresh chopped spinach

1 cup chopped mushrooms

½ precooked whole rotisserie chicken, shredded

1 tsp. salt

½ tsp. black pepper

½ tsp. dried basil

¼ tsp. red pepper flakes

1 tsp. parsley flakes

13¼-oz. box pasta, any shape or brand (I used Dreamfields)

3 cups water

1. Place the sauce in the bottom of the inner pot of the Instant Pot.

2. Add the spinach, then the mushrooms.

3. Add the chicken on top of the veggies and sauce.

4. Add the seasonings and give it a stir to mix.

5. Add the box of pasta.

6. Add the water.

7. Secure the lid and move vent to sealing. Set to Manual on high pressure for 6 minutes.

8. When cook time is up, release the pressure manually.

9. Remove the lid and stir to mix.

Chicken Stir-Fry

Hope Comerford, Clinton Township, MI

Makes 4–6 servings
Prep. Time: 5 minutes ⚬ *Cooking Time: 16 minutes*

2 lb. boneless, skinless chicken breasts

I small onion, sliced

½ cup soy sauce or Liquid Aminos

¼ cup chicken stock

I clove garlic, minced

I tsp. ginger

⅛ tsp. pepper

¼ cup cornstarch

¼ cup cold water

20-oz. bag frozen stir-fry vegetables

Cooked rice

1. Place the chicken into the inner pot of the Instant Pot, along with the onion, soy sauce, chicken stock, garlic, ginger, and pepper.

2. Secure the lid and set the vent to sealing. Manually set the cook time for 7 minutes on high pressure. (This would be a good time to start the rice on the stove, or in a second Instant Pot. See recipe on page 141 for Perfect White Rice.)

3. When cook time is up, let the pressure release naturally for 2 minutes, then release the rest of the pressure manually.

4. When the pin drops, remove the lid. Remove the chicken and shred it.

5. Switch the Instant Pot to the Sauté function. Mix the cornstarch and water in a small bowl, then stir it into the liquid in the pot. Add the frozen vegetables and continue to let things simmer and stir for another 7 minutes or so.

6. Stir the chicken back into the pot and serve over cooked rice.

Chicken and Dumplings

Bonnie Miller, Louisville, OH

Makes 4 servings
Prep. Time: 10 minutes ⚶ Cooking Time: 3 minutes

1 Tbsp. olive oil

1 small onion, chopped

2 celery stalks, cut into 1-inch pieces

6 small carrots, cut into 1-inch chunks

2 cups chicken broth

2 lb. boneless, skinless chicken breast halves, cut into 1-inch pieces

2 chicken bouillon cubes

1 tsp. salt

1 tsp. pepper

1 tsp. poultry seasoning

Biscuits:

2 cups buttermilk biscuit mix

½ cup plus 1 Tbsp. milk

1 tsp. parsley

1. Set the Instant Pot to the Sauté function and heat the olive oil.

2. Add the onion, celery, and carrots to the hot oil and sauté for 3 to 5 minutes.

3. Pour in the broth and scrape the bottom of the inner pot with a wooden spoon or spatula to deglaze. Press Cancel.

4. Add the chicken, bouillon, salt, pepper, and poultry seasoning.

5. Combine the biscuit ingredients in a bowl until just moistened. Drop 2-tablespoon mounds over the contents of the inner pot, as evenly spaced out as possible.

6. Secure the lid and set the vent to sealing. Manually set the cook time for 3 minutes.

7. When the cook time is over, manually release the pressure.

Serving suggestion:
Serve alongside Broccoli with Garlic (page 189).

Chicken Rice Bake

Nanci Keatley, Salem, OR

Makes 6 servings
Prep. Time: 8 minutes ⚜ Cooking Time: 22 minutes ⚜ Standing Time: 10 minutes

1 Tbsp. olive oil

1 cup finely diced onion

1 tsp. chopped garlic

1 cup chopped celery

2 lb. boneless, skinless chicken breasts, cut into bite-sized pieces

1 cup chopped carrots

2 cups sliced fresh mushrooms

1½ cups uncooked brown rice

1½ tsp. salt

1 tsp. pepper

1 tsp. dill weed

1½ cups low-sodium chicken broth

1. Set the Instant Pot to the Sauté function and heat the oil in the inner pot.

2. Sauté the onions and garlic for 3 minutes. Add the celery and sauté an additional 3 minutes.

3. Press Cancel. Add the chicken and spread out evenly, Add the carrots and mushrooms and spread out evenly.

4. Pour the rice evenly on top and sprinkle with the seasonings. Last, pour in the chicken broth. Do not stir.

5. Set the cook time manually to cook for 22 minutes on high pressure.

6. When the cooking time is over, manually release the pressure.

7. Allow to stand for 10 minutes before serving.

Serving suggestion:

Serve with Green Beans with Bacon (page 197).

Cheesy Chicken and Rice

Amanda Breeden, Timberville, VA

Makes 5–6 servings
Prep. Time: 5 minutes   Cooking Time: 30 minutes

3 cups low-sodium chicken broth

2 cups brown rice

1 lb. frozen boneless, skinless chicken breasts

3 cups shredded cheddar cheese

1. Add the chicken broth, rice, and frozen chicken to the inner pot of the Instant Pot.

2. Secure the lid and set the vent to sealing. Cook on high pressure setting for 30 minutes.

3. When done cooking, release the pressure manually and stir everything together.

4. Stir the cheese into the dish until it is melted and blended evenly. Serve and enjoy!

Tip:

Some like more, or less cheese. Add more if desired.

Serving suggestion:

Serve with Simple Salted Carrots (page 181).

Pot Roast

Carole Whaling, New Tripoli, PA

Makes 8 servings
Prep. Time: 20 minutes ♣ Cooking Time: 35 minutes

2 Tbsp. olive oil

3–4-lb. rump roast, or pot roast, bone removed, and cut into serving-sized pieces, trimmed of fat

4 medium potatoes, cubed or sliced

4 medium carrots, sliced

1 medium onion, sliced

1 tsp. salt

½ tsp. pepper

1 cup low-sodium beef broth

1. Press the Sauté button on the Instant Pot and add the olive oil. Once the oil is heated, lightly brown the pieces of roast, about 2 minutes on each side. Press Cancel.

2. Leave roast in Instant Pot and add the veggies around the roast, along with the salt, pepper, and beef broth.

3. Secure the lid and make sure the vent is set to sealing. Set the Instant Pot to Manual mode for 35 minutes. Let pressure release naturally when cook time is up.

Mississippi Pot Roast

Hope Comerford, Clinton Township, MI

Makes 8 servings
Prep. Time: 10–12 minutes 🍴 *Cooking Time: 60 minutes*

2 Tbsp. olive oil

3- 4-lb. chuck roast (cut into large chunks to fit the Instant Pot if necessary)

½ cup beef broth

1-oz. pkg. dry ranch seasoning

1-oz. pkg. au jus gravy mix

16-oz. jar sliced pepperoncini, with juice

Tip:

If you are pressed for time, you can skip the sauté step, but it is highly recommended.

1. Set the Instant Pot to the Sauté setting and heat the olive oil. Sear the chuck roast on all sides. This will take 8 to 10 minutes.

2. Remove the roast and set aside. Pour in the beef broth and scrape the bottom of the inner pot with a wooden spoon or spatula to scrape up any bits. Press Cancel.

3. Place the roast back in the inner pot and sprinkle with the ranch seasoning and au jus gravy mix. Pour the jar of pepperoncini over the top, including the juices.

4. Secure the lid and set the vent to sealing. Manually set the cook time for 60 minutes on high pressure.

5. When the cook time is over, let the pressure release naturally for 15 minutes, then manually release the remaining pressure.

6. When the pin drops, remove the roast and shred between 2 forks. Discard any large pieces of fat.

7. Skim off as much fat from the juice in the inner pot as possible, then stir the shredded roast back through.

Serving Suggestion:

Serve over mashed potatoes.

This is also delicious served on sub rolls with melted cheese on top, or as open-faced sandwiches.

Oui Oui French Onion Italian Style Pot Roast à la Mamma Ree

Maria Shevlin, Sicklerville, NJ

Makes 4–6 servings
Prep. Time: 15 minutes & Cooking Time: 15 minutes

2 Tbsp. olive oil

3–5-lb. pot roast

2 cups beef broth, *divided*

1 onion, chopped

4 Tbsp. butter

2 Tbsp. parsley flakes

2 tsp. onion powder

2 tsp. Italian seasoning

½ tsp. black pepper

½ tsp. paprika

2 tsp. tomato paste

2 (2-oz.) pkgs onion soup mix

1. Set the Instant Pot to the Sauté function and let it get hot. Pour in the olive oil.

2. Add the pot roast to the bottom of the inner pot and brown on both sides. Once browned, set aside momentarily.

3. Pour in ½ cup of the beef broth and deglaze the bottom of the pot, scraping up any stuck-on bits. Press Cancel, then and add the beef back in, along with the onion on top.

4. Add pats of butter, parsley flakes, onion powder, Italian seasoning, black pepper, and paprika to the top of roast and onion.

5. In a bowl, mix the tomato paste, onion soup mix, and remaining beef broth. Pour the mixture over top of the beef, seasonings, butter, and onion.

6. Secure the lid and set the vent to sealing. Manually set the cook time for 60 minutes on high pressure for a 3-pound roast, 70 minutes for a 4-pound roast, or 80 minutes for a 5-pound roast.

7. When cook time is up, let the pressure naturally release for 10 minutes, then manually release any remaining pressure.

Serving Suggestion:
Serve with egg noodles and roasted green beans.

Barbacoa

Cindy Herren, West Des Moines, IA

Makes 6–8 servings
Prep. Time: 20 minutes ⚜ Cooking Time: 60 minutes

5 cloves garlic

½ medium onion

Juice of 1 lime

2–4 Tbsp. chipotles in adobo sauce (to taste)

1 tsp. ground cumin

1 tsp. ground oregano

½ tsp. ground cloves

1 cup water

3-lb. beef eye of round or bottom round roast, all fat trimmed

2½ tsp. kosher salt

Black pepper

1 tsp. oil

3 bay leaves

½ tsp. salt, *optional*

½ tsp. cumin, *optional*

1. Place the garlic, onion, lime juice, chipotles, cumin, oregano, cloves, and water in a blender and puree until smooth.

2. Trim all the fat off the meat and then cut the meat into 3-inch pieces. Season with the salt and black pepper.

3. Set the Instant Pot to Sauté. When hot, add the oil and brown the meat in batches on all sides, about 5 minutes.

4. Press Cancel. Add all of the browned meat, sauce from the blender, and bay leaves to the inner pot.

5. Secure the lid and set the vent to sealing.

6. Cook on high pressure for 60 minutes.

7. Manually release the pressure once cook time is up.

8. Remove the meat and place in a dish. Shred with two forks, and reserve 1½ cups of the liquid. Discard the bay leaves and the remaining liquid.

9. Return the shredded meat to the pot, add ½ tsp. salt (or to taste) and ½ tsp. cumin (if using), and add the 1½ cups of the reserved liquid.

Serving Suggestion:

Serve with fresh salsa, sliced jalapeños, sour cream, and corn over Cilantro Lime Rice (page 149).

Barbecued Brisket

Dorothy Dyer, Lee's Summit, MO

Makes 9–12 servings
Prep. Time: 10 minutes ⚬ *Cooking Time: 70 minutes*

1 cup beef broth

⅓ cup Italian salad dressing

1½ tsp. liquid smoke

⅓ cup + 2 tsp. brown sugar, packed

½ tsp. celery salt

½ tsp. salt

1 Tbsp. Worcestershire sauce

½ tsp. black pepper

¼ tsp. chili powder

½ tsp. garlic powder

3–4-lb. beef brisket

1¼ cups barbecue sauce

Sandwich rolls

1. Pour the beef broth, Italian dressing, liquid smoke, brown sugar, celery salt, salt, Worcestershire sauce, pepper, chili powder, and garlic powder into the inner pot of the Instant Pot. Stir. Place the brisket into the broth mixture. You may cut it into pieces if needed for it to fit under the broth.

2. Secure the lid and set the vent to sealing. Manually set the cook time for 70 minutes on high pressure.

3. When the cook time is over, let the pressure release naturally.

4. Lift the meat out of the Instant Pot and shred it in a bowl. Pour the barbecue sauce over the meat and stir. Serve on sandwich rolls.

Serving suggestion:

Serve with Brussels Sprouts with Maple Glaze (page 199).

Korean Beef

Hope Comerford, Clinton Township, MI

Makes 8–10 servings
Prep. Time: 8–10 minutes ♣ Cooking Time: 70 minutes

I medium onion
I McIntosh apple, peeled, cored
5 cloves garlic
¼ cup rice vinegar
I tsp. gluten-free hot sauce
2 Tbsp. low-sodium gluten-free soy sauce
I Tbsp. ginger
I Tbsp. chili powder
¼ tsp. red pepper flakes
3 Tbsp. brown sugar
I cup ketchup
2–3-lb. chuck roast
I cup beef broth

1. In a food processor, puree the onion, apple, and garlic. Pour this mixture in a bowl and mix it with the rice vinegar, hot sauce, soy sauce, ginger, chili powder, red pepper flakes, brown sugar, and ketchup.

2. Place the pork roast into the bottom of the inner pot of the Instant Pot. Pour the sauce over the top and turn it so it's covered on all sides. Add the beef broth.

3. Secure the lid and set the vent to sealing. Manually set the cook time for 70 minutes on high pressure.

4. When cook time is up, let the pressure release naturally, then remove lid when the pin drops.

5. Remove the chuck roast and shred it between 2 forks. Return the shredded pork to the inner pot and mix it through the sauce.

Serving suggestion:

Serve over brown rice or quinoa with a side of bok choi sautéed in toasted sesame seed oil and red pepper flakes.

Beef with Broccoli

Anita Troyer, Fairview, MI

Makes 6 servings
Prep. Time: 15 minutes ☙ Cooking Time: 20 minutes

1 Tbsp. oil

1½ lb. boneless beef, trimmed and sliced thinly (round steak or chuck roast)

¼ tsp. black pepper

½ cup diced onion

3 cloves garlic, minced

¾ cup beef broth

½ cup soy sauce

¼ cup brown sugar

2 Tbsp. sesame oil

¼ tsp. red pepper flakes

1 lb. broccoli, chopped

3 Tbsp. water

3 Tbsp. cornstarch

1. Put oil into the inner pot of the Instant Pot and select Sauté. When oil begins to sizzle, brown the beef in several small batches, taking care to brown well. After browning, remove and put into another bowl. Season with black pepper.

2. Sauté onion in pot for 2 minutes. Add garlic and sauté another minute. Add beef broth, soy sauce, brown sugar, sesame oil, and red pepper flakes. Stir to mix well. Add beef and juices on it.

3. Add beef to mixture in inner pot. Secure lid and make sure vent is at sealing. Set on Manual at high pressure and set timer for 12 minutes.

4. After beep, turn cooker off and use quick pressure release. Remove lid.

5. In microwave bowl, steam the broccoli for 3 minutes or until desired doneness.

6. In a small bowl, stir together water and cornstarch. Add to pot and stir. Put on Sauté setting and stir some more. After mixture becomes thick, add broccoli and turn pot off.

Serving suggestion:
Serve over Perfect White Rice (page 141).

Three-Pepper Steak

Renee Hankins, Narvon, PA

Makes 10 servings
Prep. Time: 15 minutes ⚓ Cooking Time: 15 minutes

3-lb. beef flank steak, cut in ¼–½-inch-thick slices across the grain

3 bell peppers—one red, one orange, and one yellow pepper (or any combination of colors), cut into ¼-inch-thick slices

2 cloves garlic, sliced

1 large onion, sliced

1 tsp. ground cumin

½ tsp. dried oregano

1 bay leaf

¼ cup water

Salt to taste

14½-oz. can diced tomatoes in juice

Jalapeño peppers, sliced, *optional*

1. Place all ingredients into the Instant Pot and stir.

2. Sprinkle with jalapeño pepper slices, if you wish.

3. Secure the lid and make sure vent is set to sealing. Press Manual and set the time for 15 minutes.

4. When cook time is up, let the pressure release naturally for 15 minutes, then perform a quick release of the remaining pressure.

Serving Suggestion:

We love this served over noodles, rice, or torn tortillas.

Beef Goulash

Colleen Heatwole, Burton, MI

Makes 6 servings
Prep. Time: 15 minutes   ⚶   Cooking Time: 50 minutes

2 lb. beef stew meat cut into 2-inch pieces

1 large onion, chopped

3 carrots, cut into 2-inch chunks

1 medium red bell pepper, chopped

1 cup beef broth

¼ cup ketchup

2 tsp. Worcestershire sauce

2 tsp. paprika

2 tsp. minced garlic

1 tsp. salt

1. Place all the ingredients into the inner pot of the Instant Pot.

2. Secure the lid and set the vent to sealing. Manually set the cook time for 50 minutes on high pressure.

3. When the cook time is over, let the pressure release naturally for 20 minutes, then manually release the remaining pressure.

Serving Suggestion:

Mashed potatoes and green beans go well as sides, or serve with cooked barley or rice.

Beef in Noodles

Hope Comerford, Clinton Township, MI

Makes 4–6 servings
Prep. Time: 10 minutes ⚬ *Cooking Time: 38–40 minutes*

4 Tbsp. butter

1½ lb. stew beef

½ tsp. salt

¼ tsp. pepper

6 cups beef broth, *divided*

1 tsp. garlic power

1 tsp. onion powder

1 Tbsp. Worcestershire sauce

1 tsp. low-sodium soy sauce

½ cup cornstarch

½ cup cold water

24 oz. egg noodles

1. Set the Instant Pot to the Sauté function and let it get hot.

2. Melt the butter, then immediately add the beef, season with the salt and pepper, and brown on all sides.

3. Add 1 cup of the broth and deglaze the pot, scraping up any stuck-on bits. Press Cancel.

4. Add the remaining broth, garlic powder, onion powder, Worcestershire sauce, and soy sauce.

5. Secure the lid and set the vent to sealing. Manually set the cook time for 28 minutes on high pressure.

6. When cook time is up, manually release the pressure.

7. When the pin drops, remove the lid. In a small bowl, mix the cornstarch and water, then add it into the pot, stirring.

8. Stir in the egg noodles and switch the Instant Pot to the Sauté function once again. Place the lid on the pot and allow the noodles to simmer for 6–8 minutes, or until tender.

Serving suggestion:
This goes well with Brown Sugar Glazed Carrots (page 185).

Lasagna the Instant Pot Way

Hope Comerford, Clinton Township, MI

Makes 8 servings
Prep. Time: 15 minutes ✤ Cooking Time: 15 minutes

1 Tbsp. olive oil

1 lb. extra-lean ground beef or ground turkey

½ cup chopped onion

½ tsp. salt

⅛ tsp. pepper

2 cups water

12 lasagna noodles

8 oz. cottage cheese

1 egg

1 tsp. Italian seasoning

4 cups spinach, chopped or torn

1 cup sliced mushrooms

28 oz. marinara sauce

1 cup mozzarella cheese

1. Set the Instant Pot to the Sauté function and heat the olive oil. Brown the beef and onion with the salt and pepper. This will take about 5 minutes. Because you're using extra-lean ground beef, there should not be much grease, but if so, you'll need to drain it before continuing. Remove half of the ground beef and set aside. Press Cancel.

2. Pour in the water.

3. Break 4 noodles in half and arrange them on top of the beef and water.

4. Mix together the cottage cheese, egg, and Italian seasoning until the mixture is smooth. Smooth half of this mixture over the lasagna noodles.

5. Layer half of the spinach and half of the mushrooms on top.

6. Break 4 more noodles in half and lay them on top of what you just did. Spread out the remaining cottage cheese mixture.

7. Layer on the remaining spinach and mushrooms, then pour half of the marinara sauce over the top.

8. Finish with breaking the remaining 4 noodles in half and laying them on top of the previous layer. Spread the remaining marinara sauce on top.

9. Secure the lid and set the vent to sealing. Manually set the cook time for 7 minutes on high pressure.

10. When the cook time is over, let the pressure release naturally for 10 minutes, then manually release the remaining pressure.

11. When the pin drops, remove the lid and sprinkle the mozzarella cheese on top. Re-cover for 5 minutes.

12. When the 5 minutes is up, remove the lid. You can let this sit for a while to thicken up on Keep Warm.

Taco Meat

Hope Comerford, Clinton Township, MI

Makes 8 servings
Prep. Time: 10 minutes ⚬ Cooking Time: 20–25 minutes

1 Tbsp. olive oil

1 large, sweet onion, chopped

2 lb. ground sirloin

2 Tbsp. chili powder

1 Tbsp. cumin

2½ tsp. garlic powder

2½ tsp. onion powder

1 tsp. salt

½ tsp. oregano

½ tsp. red pepper flakes

2 Tbsp. water

1. Set the Instant Pot to the Sauté function. Let it get hot. Add the oil.

2. Sauté the onion for 3 minutes. Add the beef and seasonings to the inner pot and sauté until browned, about 5 minutes.

3. Add the water and scrape the bottom of the pot to bring up any stuck-on bits. Press Cancel.

4. Secure the lid and set the vent to sealing. Manually set the cook time for 15 minutes on high pressure.

5. When cook time is up, manually release the pressure. When the pin drops, remove the lid.

6. Switch the Instant Pot back to Sauté and cook off the excess liquid for 5–10 minutes.

Sausage, Carrots, Potatoes, and Cabbage

Hope Comerford, Clinton Township, MI

Makes 4 servings
Prep. Time: 5 minutes   ♣   Cooking Time: 10 minutes

1 Tbsp. olive oil

4 Tbsp. butter

1 large onion, sliced

14-oz. pkg. smoked sausage, sliced

1 cup chicken broth

2 carrots, peeled and chopped

2 lb. red potatoes, chopped

1 small head of cabbage, chopped

1½ tsp. sea salt

1½ tsp. smoked paprika

1 tsp. onion powder

¼ tsp. pepper

1. Set the Instant Pot to the Sauté function and let it get hot. Pour in the oil and butter.

2. Sauté the onion and sausage for about 4 minutes.

3. Pour in the broth and deglaze the bottom of the inner pot, scraping up any stuck-on bits. Press Cancel.

4. Add the remaining ingredients in the order listed.

5. Secure the lid and set the vent to sealing. Manually set the cook time for 6 minutes on high pressure.

6. When cook time is up, manually release the pressure.

Paprika Pork Chops with Rice

Sharon Easter, Yuba City, CA

Makes 4 servings
Prep. Time: 5 minutes ⚬ Cooking Time: 30 minutes

⅛ tsp. pepper

I tsp. paprika

4–5 thick-cut boneless pork chops
(1–1½ inches thick)

I Tbsp. olive oil

1¼ cups water, *divided*

I onion, sliced

½ green bell pepper, sliced in rings

1½ cups canned no-salt-added stewed
tomatoes

I cup brown rice

1. Mix the pepper and paprika in a flat dish. Dredge the chops in the seasoning mixture.

2. Set the Instant Pot to the Sauté function and heat the oil in the inner pot.

3. Brown the chops on both sides for 1 to 2 minutes a side. Remove the pork chops and set aside.

4. Pour a small amount of water into the inner pot and scrape up any bits from the bottom with a wooden spoon. Press Cancel.

5. Place the browned chops side by side in the inner pot. Place 1 slice onion and 1 ring of green pepper on top of each chop. Spoon tomatoes with their juices over the top.

6. Pour the rice in and pour the remaining water over the top.

7. Secure the lid and set the vent to sealing.

8. Manually set the cook time for 30 minutes on high pressure.

9. When the cooking time is over, manually release the pressure.

Serving suggestion:

This would go nicely with Dill Baby Carrots (page 183).

Pork Chops with Potatoes and Green Beans

Hope Comerford, Clinton Township, MI

Makes 4 servings
Prep. Time: 8 minutes ❧ *Cooking Time: 13 minutes*

2 Tbsp. olive oil, divided

4 boneless pork chops, 1–1½ inches thick

Salt to taste

Pepper to taste

1 cup chicken broth

2 lb. baby potatoes, sliced in half

1 lb. fresh green beans, end trimmed

3 cloves garlic, crushed

2 tsp. salt

1 tsp. onion powder

1 tsp. dried rosemary

½ tsp. dried thyme

¼ tsp. pepper

1. Set the Instant Pot to Sauté and let it get hot. Add 1 tablespoon of the oil.

2. Sprinkle each side of the pork chops with salt and pepper. Brown them on each side in the Instant Pot. Remove them when done.

3. Pour in the broth and scrape the bottom of the pot, bringing up any stuck-on bits. Press Cancel.

4. Arrange the pork chops back in the inner pot of the Instant Pot.

5. In a medium bowl, toss the potatoes and green beans with the garlic, salt, onion powder, rosemary, thyme, and pepper. Pour them over the pork chops.

6. Secure the lid and set the vent to sealing. Manually set the cook time for 8 minutes on high pressure.

7. When cook time is up, let the pressure release naturally for 10 minutes, then manually release the remaining pressure.

Pork Chops in Gravy

Hope Comerford, Clinton Township, MI

Makes 6 servings
Prep. Time: 10 minutes ⚬ *Cooking Time: 20 minutes*

1 Tbsp. olive oil

½ cup sliced onion

6 boneless pork chops, 1–1½ inches thick

Salt to taste

Pepper to taste

1½ cups beef broth, *divided*

1 tsp. Worcestershire sauce

½ tsp. low-sodium soy sauce

1 tsp. garlic powder

1 tsp. onion powder

2 tsp. cornstarch

2 tsp. cold water

½ cup sour cream

Variation:

You could add mushrooms during the sauté phase if you choose. They make a great addition.

1. Set the Instant Pot to Sauté and let it get hot. Add the oil.

2. Sauté the onion for 3 minutes.

3. Sprinkle each side of the pork chops with salt and pepper. Brown 3 of them at a time on each side in the Instant Pot. Remove them when done.

4. Pour in ½ cup of the broth and scrape the bottom of the pot, bringing up any stuck-on bits. Press Cancel.

5. Arrange the pork chops in the inner pot of the Instant Pot.

6. Pour the remaining broth, Worcestershire sauce, soy sauce, garlic powder, and onion powder over the chops.

7. Secure the lid and set the vent to sealing. Manually set the cook time for 8 minutes on high pressure.

8. When the cook time is over, let the pressure release naturally for 10 minutes, then manually release the remaining pressure.

9. When the pin drops, remove the lid. Switch the Instant Pot to Sauté.

10. Remove the chops and set aside.

11. Mix the cornstarch and cold water, then whisk into the sauce in the pot. Let thicken slightly for a few minutes. Press "Cancel."

12. Before you add the sour cream to the sauce, let it cool for a few minutes, then slowly whisk it in. Serve the chops with the gravy over the top.

Tender Tasty Ribs

Carol Eveleth, Cheyenne, WY

Makes 2–3 servings
Prep. Time: 5 minutes ⚬ Cooking Time: 35 minutes

2 tsp. salt

2 tsp. black pepper

I tsp. garlic powder

I tsp. onion powder

I slab baby back ribs

I cup water

I cup barbecue sauce, *divided*

1. Mix the salt, pepper, garlic powder, and onion powder together. Rub seasoning mixture on both sides of slab of ribs. Cut slab in half if it's too big for the Instant Pot.

2. Pour the water into the inner pot of the Instant Pot. Place the ribs into pot, drizzle with ¼ cup of sauce, and secure the lid. Make sure the vent is set to sealing.

3. Set it to Manual for 25 minutes. It will take a few minutes to heat up and seal the vent. When the cook time is over, let it sit 5 minutes, then release steam by turning valve to venting. Turn oven on to broil (or heat the grill) while you're waiting for the 5-minute resting time.

4. Remove ribs from Instant Pot and place on a baking sheet. Slather both sides with remaining ¾ cup sauce.

5. Place under broiler (or on grill) for 5–10 minutes, watching carefully so it doesn't burn. Remove and brush with a bit more sauce. Pull apart and dig in!

Serving suggestion:
This would go well with Corn on the Cob (page 179) and Potatoes with Parsley (page 165).

Carnitas

Hope Comerford, Clinton Township, MI

Makes 12 servings
Prep. Time: 10 minutes & Cooking Time: 15 minutes

2 lb. pork shoulder roast, cut into
1-inch chunks

1½ tsp. kosher salt

½ tsp. pepper

2 tsp. cumin

5 cloves garlic, minced

1 tsp. oregano

3 bay leaves

2 cups chicken stock

1 tsp. lime zest

2 Tbsp. lime juice

12 6-inch gluten-free white corn
tortillas, warmed

Sliced fresh tomato, *optional*

1. Place all ingredients, except the lime zest, lime juice, and tortillas, into the inner pot of the Instant Pot.

2. Secure the lid and set the vent to sealing. Manually set the cook time for 15 minutes on high pressure.

3. When cook time is up, let the pressure release naturally.

4. Add the lime juice and lime zest to the Inner Pot and stir. You may choose to shred the pork if you wish. Remove the bay leaves.

5. Serve on the white corn tortillas. Add tomato slices if desired.

Serving suggestion:

This would go great with Hometown Spanish Rice (page 151) and Southwestern Cauliflower (page 195).

BBQ Pork Sandwiches

Carol Eveleth, Cheyenne, WY

Makes 4 servings
Prep. Time: 20 minutes ⚓ Cooking Time: 60 minutes

2 tsp. salt

1 tsp. onion powder

1 tsp. garlic powder

2-lb. pork shoulder roast, cut into 3-inch pieces

1 Tbsp. olive oil

2 cups barbecue sauce

1. In a small bowl, combine the salt, onion powder, and garlic powder. Season the pork with the rub.

2. Turn the Instant Pot on to Sauté. Heat the olive oil in the inner pot.

3. Add the pork to the oil and turn to coat. Lock the lid and set vent to sealing.

4. Press Manual and cook on high pressure for 45 minutes.

5. When cooking is complete, release the pressure manually, then open the lid.

6. Using 2 forks, shred the pork, pour barbecue sauce over the pork, then press Sauté. Simmer, 3 to 5 minutes. Press Cancel. Toss pork to mix.

Serving suggestion:

Pile the shredded BBQ pork on the bottom half of a bun. Add any additional toppings if you wish, then finish with the top half of the bun.

Sides

Perfect White Rice

Hope Comerford, Clinton Township, MI

Makes 4 servings
Prep. Time: 2 minutes & Cooking Time: 8 minutes

1 cup uncooked white rice

1 tsp. grapeseed, olive oil, or coconut oil

1 cup water

Pinch salt

1. Rinse rice under cold running water until the water runs clear, then pour into the inner pot.

2. Add oil, water, and salt to the inner pot.

3. Lock the lid and set the steam valve to its sealing position. Select the Rice button and set to cook for 8 minutes.

4. Allow the pressure to release naturally for 10 minutes and then release any remaining pressure manually.

5. Fluff the rice with a fork and serve.

Best Brown Rice

Colleen Heatwole, Burton, MI

Makes 6–12 servings
Prep. Time: 5 minutes ⚬ Cooking Time: 22 minutes

2 cups brown rice
2½ cups water

1. Rinse brown rice in a fine-mesh strainer.

2. Add rice and water to the inner pot of the Instant Pot.

3. Secure the lid and make sure vent is on sealing.

4. Use Manual setting and select 22 minutes cooking time on high pressure.

5. When cooking time is done, let the pressure release naturally for 10 minutes, then press Cancel and manually release any remaining pressure.

Notes from the cook:

• Brown rice is my preferred rice since it is more nutritious than white rice.

• I have also cooked brown rice 25 minutes and then done a quick release and it worked fine.

• I don't add salt until it is cooked, and how much I add if any depends on how I'm using the rice.

Mushroom Risotto

Hope Comerford, Clinton Township, MI

Makes 4 servings
Prep. Time: 7 minutes ⚮ Cooking Time: 6 minutes

1 Tbsp. extra-virgin olive oil

½ cup finely chopped onion

2 cloves garlic, minced

½ cup chopped baby bella mushrooms

½ cup chopped shiitake mushrooms

¼ tsp. salt

⅛ tsp. pepper

1 cup uncooked arborio rice

2 cups low-sodium chicken stock

½ cup frozen peas, thawed

¼ cup freshly grated low-fat Parmesan cheese

1 Tbsp. butter or margarine, *optional*

1. Set the Instant Pot to the Sauté function and heat the oil in the inner pot.

2. Sauté the onion and garlic for 3 minutes. Add the mushrooms, salt, and pepper, and continue sautéing for an additional 3 to 4 minutes.

3. Press Cancel. Stir in the rice and chicken stock. Secure the lid and set the vent to sealing.

4. Manually set the cook time for 6 minutes on high pressure.

5. When the cooking time is over, manually release the pressure.

6. When the pin drops, remove the lid and stir in the peas, grated Parmesan, and butter or margarine (if using). Let the peas heat through for about 2 minutes, then serve.

Herbed Rice Pilaf

Betty K. Drescher, Quakertown, PA

Makes 6 servings
Prep. Time: 10 minutes ✿ *Cooking Time: 22 minutes*

1 Tbsp. olive oil

½ cup chopped onion

1 cup chopped celery

1½ cups raw brown rice

1¾ cups low-sodium, fat-free chicken broth

¾ tsp. Worcestershire sauce

¾ tsp. low-sodium soy sauce

¾ tsp. dried oregano

¾ tsp. dried thyme

1. Set the Instant Pot to the Sauté function and heat the oil in the inner pot.

2. Add the onion and celery to the inner pot and sauté for about 5 minutes. Add the rice and lightly toast, about 1 minute. Press Cancel.

3. Add the broth, Worcestershire sauce, soy sauce, oregano, and thyme. Secure the lid and set the vent to sealing.

4. Manually set the time for 22 minutes on high pressure.

5. When the cooking time is over, let the pressure release naturally.

6. When the pin drops, remove the lid and fluff the rice with a fork. Serve and enjoy!

Cilantro Lime Rice

Cindy Herren, West Des Moines, IA

Makes 6–8 servings

Prep. Time: 5 minutes ⚬ *Cooking Time: 3 minutes*

2 cups extra-long grain rice or jasmine rice

4 cup water

2 Tbsp. olive oil or butter, *divided*

2 tsp. salt

¼ cup fresh chopped cilantro

1 lime, juiced

1. Add the rice, the water, 1 tablespoon of the oil, and the salt to the inner pot of the Instant Pot and stir.

2. Secure the lid and set the vent to sealing.

3. Manually set the cook time to 3 minutes on high pressure.

4. When the cooking time is over, let the pressure release naturally for 10 minutes, then manually release the remaining pressure.

5. When the pin drops, remove the lid. Fluff the rice with a fork. Add the chopped cilantro, lime juice, and remaining oil and mix well.

Serving Suggestion:

Serve with Barbacoa (page 107).

Hometown Spanish Rice

Beverly Flatt-Getz, Warriors Mark, PA

Makes 6–8 servings
Prep. Time: 8 minutes   Cooking Time: 3 minutes

1 Tbsp. olive oil

1 large onion, chopped

1 bell pepper, chopped

2 cups long-grain rice, rinsed

1½ cups low-sodium chicken stock

28-oz. can low-sodium stewed tomatoes

Grated Parmesan cheese, *optional*

1. Set the Instant Pot to Sauté and heat the oil in the inner pot.

2. Sauté the onion and bell pepper in the inner pot for about 3–5 minutes.

3. Add the rice and continue to sauté for about 1 more minute. Press Cancel.

4. Add the chicken stock and tomatoes with their juices into the inner pot, in that order.

5. Secure the lid and set the vent to sealing.

6. Manually set the cook time for 3 minutes on high pressure.

7. When the cooking time is over, let the pressure release naturally for 10 minutes, then manually release the remaining pressure.

8. When the pin drops, remove the lid. Fluff the rice with a fork.

9. Sprinkle with Parmesan cheese, if using, just before serving.

Cheesy Broccoli Rice Casserole

Hope Comerford, Clinton Township, MI

Makes 4 servings
Prep. Time: 10 minutes & *Cooking Time: 6 minutes*

1 Tbsp. olive oil

¾ cup chopped onion

4-oz. fresh sliced mushrooms

2 cups rice

1 tsp. garlic powder

1 tsp. salt

¼ tsp. pepper

2½ cups chicken broth, *divided*

2 cups chopped broccoli florets

1½ cups shredded cheddar cheese

1. Set the Instant Pot to Sauté mode and heat the oil.

2. Sauté the onion and mushrooms in the oil for about 3 minutes. Press Cancel.

3. Add the rice, garlic powder, salt, pepper, and 2 cups of the broth. Stir.

4. Secure the lid and set the vent to sealing. Manually set the cook time for 5 minutes on high pressure.

5. When the cook time is over, manually release the pressure. When the pin drops, remove the lid.

6. Stir in the broccoli and remaining ½ cup of broth.

7. Secure the lid and set the vent to sealing. Manually set the cook time for 1 minute on high pressure.

8. When the cook time is over, manually release the pressure.

9. When the pin drops, remove the lid and stir in the cheese.

Quinoa with Apples and Cranberries

Colleen Heatwole, Burton, MI

Makes 4 servings
Prep. Time: 5 minutes ⚬ Cooking Time: 2 minutes

1 cup quinoa, rinsed well

½ cup roasted slivered almonds

1 bouillon cube, chicken or beef

1½ cups water

¼ tsp. salt, *optional*

1 cinnamon stick

½ cup dried cranberries or cherries

1 cup peeled and chopped apples

1 bay leaf

1. Add all ingredients to the inner pot of the Instant Pot.

2. Secure the lid and make sure vent is on sealing. Cook 2 minutes using high pressure in Manual mode.

3. Turn off pot and let the pressure release naturally for 10 minutes. After 10 minutes are up, release pressure manually.

4. Remove cinnamon stick and bay leaf.

5. Fluff with fork and serve.

Baked Potatoes

Hope Comerford, Clinton Township, MI

Makes 4–6 servings
Prep. Time: 5 minutes ⚬ Cooking Time: 12–20 minutes

1 cup cold water

4–6 russet potatoes

1. Place the trivet into the bottom of the inner pot of the Instant Pot.

2. Pour in the cup of cold water.

3. Wash/scrub each potato, then pierce each all over with a fork.

4. Place the potatoes on top of the trivet.

5. Secure the lid and set the vent to sealing. Set the cook time manually according to the chart below:

Small Russet Potatoes	12 minutes
Medium Russet Potatoes	14 minutes
Large Russet Potatoes	16 minutes
Extra-Large Russet Potatoes	18 minutes

6. When cook time is up, let the pressure release naturally. Test the potatoes with a fork. If you're not able to easily poke into the flesh, then reseal the lid and set it for 2 more minutes of cook time.

Perfect Sweet Potatoes

Brittney Horst, Lititz, PA

Makes 4–6 servings

Prep. Time: 5 minutes ☙ Cooking Time: 15 minutes

4–6 medium sweet potatoes

1 cup of water

1. Scrub skin of sweet potatoes with a brush until clean. Pour water into inner pot of the Instant Pot.

2. Place steamer basket in the bottom of the inner pot. Place sweet potatoes on top of steamer basket.

3. Secure the lid and turn valve to seal.

4. Select the Manual mode and set to pressure cook on high for 15 minutes.

5. Allow pressure to release naturally (about 10 minutes).

6. Once the pressure valve lowers, remove lid and serve immediately.

Note:

You can store cooked sweet potatoes in the fridge for 3–4 days in an airtight container.

Tip:

Super large sweet potatoes need more than 15 minutes! I tried one mega sweet potato and it was not cooked in the center. Maybe 20 minutes will do.

Mashed Potatoes

Colleen Heatwole, Burton, MI

Makes 3–4 servings
Prep. Time: 10 minutes ☙ *Cooking Time: 5 minutes*

1 cup water

6 medium potatoes, peeled and quartered

2 Tbsp. unsalted butter

½–¾ cup milk, warmed

Salt and pepper to taste

1. Add 1 cup water to the inner pot of the Instant Pot. Put the steamer basket in the pot and place potatoes in the basket.

2. Seal the lid and make sure vent is at sealing. Using Manual mode, select 5 minutes cook time, high pressure.

3. When cook time ends, do a manual release. Use a fork to test potatoes. If needed, relock lid and cook at high pressure a few minutes more.

4. Transfer potatoes to large mixing bowl. Mash using hand mixer, stirring in butter. Gradually add warmed milk. Season with salt and pepper to taste.

Note:

A few lumps are okay . . . that lets you know they are real potatoes. Some people prefer a ricer to a hand mixer for perfect, lump-free mashed potatoes. I used to do it that way, but my family is fine with hand-mixer mashed potatoes.

Scalloped Potatoes

Hope Comerford, Clinton Township, MI

Makes 8–10 servings
Prep. Time: 15 minutes & Cooking Time: 1 minute & Baking Time: 15 minutes

3 lb. white potatoes, peeled or unpeeled and sliced into 4-inch-thick slices

1 cup chicken broth

1 tsp. garlic powder

½ tsp. salt

¼ tsp. pepper

½ cup heavy cream

Nonstick cooking spray

¼ lb. bacon, cut in 1-inch squares, browned until crisp, and drained

2 cups shredded cheddar cheese

1. Place the potato slices, broth, garlic powder, salt, and pepper in the inner pot of the Instant Pot.

2. Secure the lid and set the vent to sealing. Manually set the cook time for 1 minutes.

3. When the cook time is over, let the pressure release naturally for 3 minutes, then manually release the remaining pressure.

4. When the pin drops, remove the lid. Drain the potatoes, reserving the liquid. Set the potatoes aside for a moment, and return the liquid back to the inner pot.

5. Set the Instant Pot to the Sauté function. Stir in the heavy cream. Let the mixture simmer for a couple minutes.

6. Preheat the oven to 375°F.

7. Spray a 7-inch round baking dish or pie dish with nonstick cooking spray. Layer in half of the potatoes, half of the bacon, half of the cheese, and half of the cream sauce. Repeat this process with the remaining potatoes, bacon, cheese, and sauce.

8. Place the baking dish into the oven for 15 minutes, or until bubbly.

Potatoes with Parsley

Colleen Heatwole, Burton, MI

Makes 4 servings
Prep. Time: 10 minutes ♣ Cooking Time: 5 minutes

3 Tbsp. margarine, *divided*

2 lb. medium red potatoes (about 2 oz. each), halved lengthwise

1 clove garlic, minced

½ tsp. salt

½ cup low-sodium chicken broth

2 Tbsp. chopped fresh parsley

1. Place 1 Tbsp. margarine in the inner pot of the Instant Pot and select Sauté.

2. After margarine is melted, add potatoes, garlic, and salt, stirring well.

3. Sauté 4 minutes, stirring frequently.

4. Add chicken broth and stir well.

5. Seal lid, make sure vent is on sealing, then select Manual for 5 minutes on high pressure.

6. When cooking time is up, manually release the pressure.

7. Strain potatoes, toss with remaining margarine and chopped parsley, and serve immediately.

Bacon Ranch Red Potatoes

Hope Comerford, Clinton Township, MI

Makes 6 servings
Prep. Time: 15 minutes   Cooking Time: 7 minutes

4 strips bacon, chopped into small pieces

2 lb. red potatoes, diced

1 Tbsp. fresh chopped parsley

1 tsp. sea salt

4 cloves garlic, chopped

1-oz. packet ranch dressing/seasoning mix

⅓ cup water

½ cup shredded sharp white cheddar

2 Tbsp. chopped green onions for garnish

1. Set the Instant Pot to Sauté, add the bacon to the inner pot, and cook until crisp.

2. Stir in the potatoes, parsley, sea salt, garlic, ranch dressing/seasoning mix, and water.

3. Secure the lid, make sure vent is at sealing, then set the Instant Pot to Manual for 7 minutes at high pressure.

4. When cooking time is up, do a quick release and carefully open the lid.

5. Stir in the cheese. Garnish with the green onions.

Hope's Potato Salad

Hope Comerford, Clinton Township, MI

Makes 8 servings
Prep. Time: 30 minutes ☙ *Cooking Time: 4 minutes*

1 ½ cups water
6 russet potatoes, peeled and cubed
4 eggs, washed
1 cup mayonnaise
1 Tbsp. yellow mustard
2 tsp. garlic powder
2 tsp. onion powder
1 ½ tsp. salt
¼ tsp. pepper
½ cup chopped onion
¼ cup diced celery
½ cup chopped sweet pickles, *optional*

1. Pour the water into the inner pot of the Instant Pot and place a steamer basket on top.

2. Put the cubed potatoes into the steamer basket and place the eggs on top.

3. Secure the lid and set the vent to sealing. Manually set the cook time for 4 minutes on high pressure.

4. When cook time is up, manually release the pressure and turn the pot off.

5. Remove the lid. Place the eggs into a bowl of ice water. Remove the potatoes and let cool.

6. When the eggs have cooled a bit, peel them and separate the whites from the yolks, then chop the yolks.

7. In a large bowl, mash the yolks with the mayonnaise, mustard, garlic powder, onion powder, salt, and pepper. Mix well.

8. Add the cooled potatoes, onion, celery and sweet pickles if using. Stir well.

9. Refrigerate for at least 4 hours before serving.

Perfect Pinto Beans

Hope Comerford, Clinton Township, MI

Makes 8 servings
Prep. Time: 2 minutes & Cooking Time: 50 minutes

1 large onion, chopped

1 lb. dry pinto beans, sorted and rinsed

6 cups vegetable or chicken broth

2 bay leaves

1 ½ tsp. sea salt

1 tsp. cumin

½ tsp. paprika

¼ tsp. pepper

1. Place all ingredients into the inner pot of the Instant Pot.

2. Secure the lid and set the vent to sealing. Manually set the cook time for 50 minutes on high pressure.

3. When the cook time is over, let the pressure release naturally for 15 minutes, then manually release the remaining pressure. Remove the bay leaves before serving.

Baked Pinto Beans

Janie Steele, Moore, OK

Makes 8 servings
Prep. Time: 15 minutes   ♨   Cooking Time: 90 minutes

1 lb. dry pinto beans

1 Tbsp. salt

6 cups water

6 slices bacon, diced

1 onion, diced

¾ cup molasses

½ cup brown sugar

1½ tsp. dry mustard

¾ cup ketchup

½ tsp. salt

½ tsp. garlic

1½ tsp. white wine vinegar

½ tsp. chili powder

½ tsp. Worcestershire sauce

1. Put beans, salt, and water in the inner pot of the Instant Pot.

2. Secure the lid and make sure vent is at sealing. Press the Bean/Chili setting and set on normal for 60 minutes.

3. Let the pressure release naturally, then drain the beans. Remove the beans from the pot and set aside.

4. Sauté the bacon and onion in inner pot until the bacon is crisp and onion is translucent.

5. Mix seasonings in a bowl

6. Return beans to pot; stir.

7. Pour seasonings over beans, then stir.

8. Secure the lid and make sure vent is at sealing. Press the Bean/Chili setting and set for 30 minutes.

9. Let pressure release naturally then remove lid. Let sit to thicken.

Black Beans

Hope Comerford, Clinton Township, MI

Makes 10 servings
Prep. Time: 10 minutes ⚬ Cooking Time: 25 minutes

I lb. dry black beans
I cup chopped onion
3 cloves garlic
2 tsp. sea salt
¼ tsp. pepper
4 cups vegetable broth
2 cups water

1. Pick through the beans to make sure there are no rocks or other debris, then rinse them well.

2. Place the beans, onion, garlic, sea salt, and pepper into the inner pot of the Instant Pot.

3. Pour the broth and water over the top.

4. Secure the lid and set the vent to sealing. Manually set the cook time for 25 minutes on high pressure.

5. When cook time is up, let the pressure release naturally.

Instant Pot Spaghetti Squash

Hope Comerford, Clinton Township, MI

Makes 4–6 servings
Prep. Time: 5 minutes ❧ Cooking Time: 10 minutes

1 medium spaghetti squash
1 cup water

Serving Suggestions:

- Serve with a little bit of butter or margarine and a touch of salt and pepper. Add red pepper flakes for some spice.
- Serve as a delicious and healthy alternative in dishes that use traditional spaghetti noodles.

1. Cut the spaghetti squash in the middle (not lengthwise) so that it will fit in the inner pot.

2. Pour the water into the inner pot of the Instant Pot and place the trivet on top.

3. Place the squash pieces, cut-side down, on the trivet.

4. Secure the lid and set the vent to sealing.

5. Manually set the cook time for 10 minutes on high pressure.

6. When the cooking time is over, manually release the pressure.

7. When the pin drops, remove the lid.

8. Carefully remove the squash, and, using a fork, shred the squash inside the skin. To do this, move your fork clockwise around the inside of the squash.

Corn on the Cob

Hope Comerford, Clinton Township, MI

Makes 6 servings
Prep. Time: 10 minutes ⚭ *Cooking Time: 2 minutes*

I cup water

6 small ears of corn, husked and ends
cut off

1. Place the trivet in the bottom of the Instant Pot and pour in the water.

2. Place the ears of corn inside.

3. Seal the lid and make sure vent is set to sealing. Press Manual and set time for 2 minutes.

4. When cook time is up, release the pressure manually.

Simple Salted Carrots

Hope Comerford, Clinton Township, MI

Makes 4 servings
Prep. Time: 5 minutes   Cooking Time: 2 minutes

1 lb. pkg. baby carrots
1 cup water
1 Tbsp. margarine
Sea salt to taste

1. Combine the carrots and water in the inner pot of the Instant Pot.

2. Seal the lid and make sure the vent is on sealing. Select Manual for 2 minutes.

3. When cooking time is done, release the pressure manually, then pour the carrots into a strainer.

4. Wipe the inner pot dry. Select the Sauté function and add the margarine.

5. When the margarine is melted, add the carrots back into the inner pot and sauté them until they are coated well with the margarine.

6. Remove the carrots and sprinkle them with the sea salt to taste before serving.

Dill Baby Carrots

Melanie Mohler, Ephrata, PA

Makes 4–5 servings
Prep. Time: 5 minutes ⚥ Cooking Time: 5 minutes

I cup water
I lb. baby carrots
I Tbsp. olive oil
I Tbsp. dried dill weed
¼ tsp. of salt

1. Pour the water into the inner pot of the Instant Pot.

2. Place the steamer basket into the pot and pour the carrots into it.

3. Secure the lid and set the vent to sealing. Manually set the cook time for 2 minutes on high pressure.

4. When cook time is up, manually release the pressure. Carefully remove the basket and set the carrots aside. Discard water in the pot and wipe dry.

5. Switch the Instant Pot to the Sauté function. When it is hot, add the olive oil.

6. Sauté the carrots, dill, and salt for 2–3 minutes.

Brown Sugar Glazed Carrots

Michele Ruvola, Vestal, NY

Makes 10 servings
Prep. Time: 5 minutes ⚬ Cooking Time: 4 minutes

32-oz. bag baby carrots
½ cup vegetable broth
½ cup brown sugar
4 Tbsp. butter
½ Tbsp. salt

1. Place all ingredients in inner pot of the Instant Pot.

2. Secure the lid, turn valve to sealing, and set timer for 4 minutes on Manual at high pressure.

3. When cooking time is up, perform a quick release to release pressure.

4. Stir carrots, then serve.

Steamed Broccoli

Hope Comerford, Clinton Township, MI

Makes 4–6 servings
Prep. Time: 5 minutes   Cooking Time: 0-1 minute

1 cup water or vegetable broth

1 small or medium head of broccoli, cut into florets and rinsed

1. Pour the water or broth into the inner pot.

2. Place a steamer basket into the inner pot of the Instant Pot, then place the broccoli florets inside it.

3. Secure the lid and set the vent to sealing. Manually set the cook time for 0–1 minutes. If you like your broccoli on the crip side, set for 0 minutes. If you like it more tender, set the cook time for 1 minute.

4. When cook time is up, manually release the pressure.

Broccoli with Garlic

Andrea Cunningham, Arlington, KS

Makes 4 servings
Prep. Time: 5 minutes & Cooking Time: 0 minutes

½ cup cold water

1 head (about 5 cups) broccoli, cut into long pieces all the way through (you will eat the stems)

1 Tbsp. olive oil

2–3 cloves garlic, sliced thin

⅛ tsp. pepper

Lemon wedges

1. Place a steamer basket into the inner pot along with the cold water. Put the broccoli into the steamer basket.

2. Secure the lid and set the vent to sealing.

3. Manually set the cook time for 0 minutes on high pressure.

4. Manually release the pressure when it's done. Press Cancel.

5. When the pin drops, open the lid and place the broccoli into an ice bath or run under cold water to stop it from cooking. Let it air dry.

6. Carefully remove the water from the inner pot and wipe it dry.

7. Set the Instant Pot to the Sauté function and heat the oil.

8. Sauté the garlic for 1 minute, then add the broccoli, sprinkle it with the pepper, and continue to sauté for an additional 1 to 2 minutes.

9. Just before serving, squeeze lemon juice over the top.

Steamed Cauliflower

Hope Comerford, Clinton Township, MI

Makes 6–8 servings
Prep. Time: 5 minutes ⚶ Cooking Time: 1 minute

I cup water

I large head of cauliflower, cut into florets

Salt and pepper

1. Pour the water into the inner pot of the Instant Pot, then place the steamer basket on top.

2. Put the cauliflower florets into the steamer basket.

3. Secure the lid and set the vent to sealing. Manually set the cook time for 1 minute on high pressure.

4. When cook time is up, manually release the pressure.

5. When the pin drops, remove the lid, add salt and pepper to taste, and serve.

Garlic Butter Cauliflower

Hope Comerford, Clinton Township, MI

Makes 6–8 servings
Prep. Time: 5 minutes ⚘ Cooking Time: 4–5 minutes

1 cup water

1 large head of cauliflower, cut into florets

½ cup butter

4 garlic gloves, crushed

½ tsp. salt

⅛ tsp. pepper

1. Pour the water into the inner pot of the Instant Pot, then place the steamer basket on top.

2. Put the cauliflower florets into the steamer basket.

3. Secure the lid and set the vent to sealing. Manually set the cook time for 1 minute on high pressure.

4. When cook time is up, manually release the pressure. Carefully remove the basket and discard the water from the inner pot. Wipe it dry.

5. Switch the Instant Pot to the Sauté function and let it get hot.

6. Add the butter to the inner pot and let melt. Once melted, add the garlic, cauliflower, salt, and pepper. Sauté for 2–3 minutes.

Southwestern Cauliflower

Hope Comerford, Clinton Township, MI

Makes 6–8 servings
Prep. Time: 5 minutes   Cooking Time: 1 minute

1 cup water

1 large head of cauliflower, cut into florets

1 Tbsp. olive oil

½ tsp. smoked paprika

½ tsp. chili powder

½ tsp. cumin

½ tsp. sea salt

¼ tsp. oregano

⅛ tsp. black pepper

1. Pour the water into the inner pot of the Instant Pot, then place the steamer basket on top.

2. Put the cauliflower florets into a medium-sized bowl and pour over the olive oil and sprinkle the seasonings over the top. Toss to coat everything well. Pour into the steamer basket.

3. Secure the lid and set the vent to sealing. Manually set the cook time for 1 minute on high pressure.

4. When cook time is up, manually release the pressure.

5. When the pin drops, carefully remove the lid and serve the cauliflower.

Green Beans with Bacon

Hope Comerford, Clinton Township, MI

Makes 6 servings
Prep. Time: 7 minutes ⚙ Cooking Time: 5 minutes

Nonstick cooking spray

5 slices thick-cut bacon, chopped

½ cup chopped red onion

4 cloves garlic, chopped

¾ cups chicken stock

½ tsp. sea salt

⅛ tsp. pepper

⅛ tsp. red pepper flakes

1½ lb. fresh green beans, ends snipped and cut in half

1. Set the Instant Pot to the Sauté function and let it get nice and hot. Spray the inner pot with nonstick cooking spray and then add the bacon. Sauté until crispy.

2. Add the onion and garlic to the inner pot and sauté for an additional 2–3 minutes.

3. Pour in the chicken stock and scrape the bottom of the inner pot with a wooden spoon or spatula, bringing up any stuck on bits. Press Cancel.

4. Pour in the remaining ingredients.

5. Secure the lid and set the vent to sealing. Manually set the cook time for 5 minutes on high pressure.

6. When the cook time is over, manually release the pressure.

Brussels Sprouts with Maple Glaze

Hope Comerford, Clinton Township, MI

Makes 6 servings
Prep. Time: 5–6 minutes ⚬ *Cooking Time: 3 minutes*

Nonstick cooking spray
4 slices thick-cut bacon, chopped
1 shallot, diced
½ cup chicken broth
1 lb. Brussels sprouts, halved if large
⅓ cup light brown sugar
1½ Tbsp. Dijon mustard
2 Tbsp. maple syrup

1. Set the Instant Pot to the Sauté function and let it get nice and hot. Spray the inner pot with nonstick cooking spray and then add the bacon. Sauté until crispy.

2. Add the shallot and sauté for 1 more minute.

3. Pour in the chicken broth and scrape the bottom of the pot with a wooden spoon or spatula. Press Cancel.

4. Pour in the Brussels sprouts and secure the lid. Set the vent to sealing.

5. Manually set the cook time for 3 minutes. When the cook time is over, manually release the pressure.

6. When the pin drops, remove the lid.

7. In a medium bowl, mix together the brown sugar, Dijon mustard, and maple syrup.

8. Remove the contents of the inner pot with a slotted spoon into the bowl with the maple glaze. Toss and serve.

Desserts

Lemon Pudding Cake

Jean Butzer, Batavia, NY

Makes 6 servings
Prep. Time: 15 minutes & Cooking Time: 50 minutes

3 eggs, separated
1 tsp. grated lemon zest
¼ cup lemon juice
1 Tbsp. melted, soft tub margarine
1½ cups nonfat half-and-half
½ cup sugar plus 2 Tbsp. sugar
¼ cup flour
⅛ tsp. salt
1 cup water

1. Beat the egg whites until stiff peaks form. Set aside.

2. Beat the egg yolks. Blend in the lemon zest, lemon juice, margarine, and half-and-half.

3. In separate bowl, combine the sugar, flour, and salt. Add to egg-lemon mixture, beating until smooth.

4. Fold into beaten egg whites.

5. Spoon into a greased and floured 7-inch springform pan. Cover with foil.

6. Place the trivet into the Instant Pot with the water. Place a foil sling on top of the trivet, then place the springform pan on top of the trivet.

7. Secure the lid and make sure lid is set to sealing. Press Manual and set time for 40 minutes.

8. Perform a quick release of the pressure when cooking time is done. Remove the springform pan carefully using hot pads with the foil sling and let cool on a cooling rack.

Dump Cake

Janice Muller, Derwood, MD

Makes 15 servings
Prep. Time: 20 minutes ⚬ *Cooking Time: 50 minutes*

8-oz. can crushed pineapple

20-oz. can blueberry or cherry pie filling

¾ of a 15.2-oz. pkg. yellow cake mix

Sprinkle of cinnamon

⅓ cup light soft tub margarine

⅓ cup chopped walnuts

1 cup water

1. Grease bottom and sides of a 7-inch springform pan or cake pan.

2. Spread layers of pineapple, blueberry pie filling, and dry cake mix. Be careful not to mix the layers.

3. Sprinkle with cinnamon.

4. Top with thin layers of margarine chunks and nuts.

5. Cover the pan with foil.

6. Place the trivet into your Instant Pot and pour in 1 cup of water. Place a foil sling on top of the trivet, then place the springform pan on top.

7. Secure the lid and make sure lid is set to sealing. Press Steam and set for 50 minutes.

8. When cook time is up, release the pressure manually, then carefully remove the springform pan by using hot pads to lift the pan up by the foil sling. Place on a cooling rack until cool.

Variation:

Use a package of spice cake mix and apple pie filling.

Carrot Cake

Colleen Heatwole, Burton, MI

Makes 10 servings
Prep. Time: 35 minutes ⚬ Cooking Time: 50 minutes

⅓ cup canola oil

2 eggs

I Tbsp. hot water

½ cup grated raw carrots

¾ cup flour and 2 Tbsp. flour, *divided*

¾ cup sugar

½ tsp. baking powder

⅛ tsp. salt

¼ tsp. ground allspice

½ tsp. ground cinnamon

⅛ tsp. ground cloves

½ cup chopped nuts

½ cup raisins or chopped dates

I cup water

1. In a large bowl, beat the oil, eggs, and hot water for 1 minute.

2. Add the carrots. Mix well.

3. Stir together the ¾ cup flour, sugar, baking powder, salt, allspice, cinnamon, and cloves. Add to the creamed mixture.

4. Toss the nuts and raisins in a bowl with 2 tablespoons of flour. Add to creamed mixture. Mix well.

5. Pour into greased and floured 7-inch springform pan and cover with foil.

6. Place the trivet into the Instant Pot and pour in the water. Place a foil sling on top of the trivet, then place the springform pan on top.

7. Secure the lid and make sure lid is set to sealing. Press Steam and set for 50 minutes.

8. When the cook time is over, release the pressure manually, then carefully remove the springform pan by using hot pads to lift the pan up by the foil sling. Place on a cooling rack until cool.

Chocolate Bundt Cake

Margaret Wenger Johnson, Keezletown, VA

Makes 10 servings
Prep. Time: 15 minutes ⚜ Cooking Time: 30 minutes ⚜ Cooling Time: 20 minutes

1½ cups whole wheat pastry flour

½ cup turbinado sugar, or sugar of your choice

1½ Tbsp. unsweetened cocoa powder

¼ tsp. salt

1⅛ tsp. baking soda

½ Tbsp. vanilla extract

1 Tbsp. white vinegar

¼ cup canola oil

1 cup boiling water

1 cup room-temperature water

1. In a mixing bowl, sift together the flour, sugar, cocoa powder, salt, and baking soda.

2. Make 3 holes in the dry ingredients. Pour the vanilla, vinegar, and oil into those holes.

3. Add the boiling water. Beat for 2 minutes by hand, or with a mixer. (This will make a thin batter.)

4. Pour the batter into a greased 7-inch nonstick Bundt pan. Cover with foil.

5. Pour the room-temperature water into the inner pot of the Instant Pot and place the trivet on top.

6. Place the covered Bundt pan on top of the trivet in the inner pot. Secure the lid and set the vent to sealing.

7. Manually set the cook time for 30 minutes on high pressure.

8. When the cooking time is over, let the pressure release naturally.

9. When the pin drops, remove the lid and carefully remove the trivet with oven mitts.

10. Remove the foil and let the cake cool for about 20 minutes.

Tip:

You may exchange the canola oil for coconut oil if you wish.

Strawberry Shortcake

Joanna Harrison, Lafayette, CO

Makes 8 servings
Prep. Time: 25 minutes   ❧   Cooking Time: 40 minutes   ❧   Cooling Time: 7 minutes

1 qt. (4 cups) fresh strawberries

3 Tbsp. agave syrup or honey, *divided*

1½ cups whole wheat pastry flour

1 tsp. baking powder

⅛ tsp. salt

¼ cup trans-fat-free buttery spread

Egg substitute equivalent to 1 egg, or 2 egg whites

½ cup nonfat milk

1 cup water

1. Mash or slice the strawberries in a bowl. Stir in 2 tablespoons agave syrup. Set aside and refrigerate.

2. In a large mixing bowl, combine the flour, baking powder, salt, and 1 tablespoon agave syrup.

3. Cut the buttery spread into the dry ingredients with a pastry cutter or 2 knives until crumbly.

4. In a small bowl, beat the egg substitute and milk together.

5. Stir the wet ingredients into the flour mixture just until moistened.

6. Pour the batter into a greased 7-inch Bundt pan. Cover tightly with foil.

7. Pour the water into the inner pot and place the trivet on top. Place the Bundt pan on top of the trivet in the inner pot. Secure the lid and set the vent to sealing.

8. Manually set the cook time for 40 minutes on high pressure.

9. When cooking time is up, allow the pressure to release naturally for 10 minutes, then manually release the remaining pressure.

10. When the pin drops, remove the lid and carefully lift the trivet out of the inner pot with oven mitts.

11. Allow cake to cool to cool in the pan for 7 minutes, then remove onto the cooling rack.

12. Cut the cake into desired serving and spoon berries over the top.

Black and Blue Cobbler

Renee Shirk, Mount Joy, PA

Makes 12 servings
Prep. Time: 30 minutes ⚘ *Cooking Time: 15 minutes*

I cup flour

12 Tbsp. sugar, *divided*

Sugar substitute to equal 6 Tbsp. sugar, *divided*

I tsp. baking powder

¼ tsp. salt

¼ tsp. ground cinnamon

¼ tsp. ground nutmeg

2 eggs, beaten

2 Tbsp. milk

2 Tbsp. vegetable oil

2 cups fresh, or frozen, blueberries

2 cups fresh, or frozen, blackberries

¾ cup water

I tsp. grated orange peel

I cup water

Whipped topping or ice cream, *optional*

1. Combine flour, 6 Tbsp. sugar, sugar substitute equal to 3 Tbsp. sugar, baking powder, salt, cinnamon, and nutmeg.

2. Combine eggs, milk, and oil. Stir into dry ingredients until moistened.

3. Spread the batter evenly over bottom of greased 1½-quart baking dish.

4. In a saucepan, combine berries, water, orange peel, and remaining sugar, and sugar substitute. Bring to boil. Remove from heat and pour over batter. Cover with foil.

5. Place the trivet into your Instant Pot and pour in the water. Place a foil sling on top of the trivet, then place the baking dish on top.

6. Secure the lid and make sure lid is set to sealing. Press Manual and set for 35 minutes.

7. When cook time is up, allow the pressure to release naturally for 10 minutes, then release the remaining pressure manually. Carefully remove the baking dish by using hot pads to lift the foil sling. Place on a cooling rack, uncovered, for 30 minutes.

8. Serve with whipped topping or ice cream (if using).

Creamy Orange Cheesecake

Jeanette Oberholtzer, Manheim, PA

Makes 10 servings
Prep. Time: 35 minutes   ♣   Cooking Time: 35 minutes
Cooling Time: 2 or more hours   ♣   Chilling Time: 8 hours

Crust:

¾ cup graham cracker crumbs

2 Tbsp. sugar

3 Tbsp. melted soft tub margarine

Filling:

2 (8-oz.) pkg. cream cheese, at room temperature

⅔ cup sugar

2 eggs

1 egg yolk

¼ cup frozen orange juice concentrate

1 tsp. orange zest

1 Tbsp. flour

½ tsp. vanilla extract

1½ cups water

1. Combine crust ingredients. Pat into 7-inch springform pan.

2. Cream together the cream cheese and sugar. Add the eggs and yolk. Beat for 3 minutes.

3. Beat in the juice, zest, flour, and vanilla. Beat 2 minutes.

4. Pour the batter into the crust. Cover with foil.

5. Place the trivet into the Instant Pot and pour in the water. Place a foil sling on top of the trivet, then place the springform pan on top.

6. Secure the lid and make sure lid is set to sealing. Press Manual and set for 35 minutes.

7. When the cook time is over, press Cancel and allow the pressure to release naturally for 7 minutes, then release the remaining pressure manually.

8. Carefully remove the springform pan by using hot pads to lift the pan up by the foil sling. Uncover and place on a cooling rack until cool, then refrigerate for 8 hours.

Buttery Rice Pudding

Janie Steele, Moore, OK

Makes 6–8 servings
Prep. Time: 5 minutes ⚮ *Cooking Time: 14 minutes*

1½ Tbsp. butter

1 cup uncooked rice

½ cup sugar

1 cup water

2 cups milk (2% works best)

1 egg

¼ cup evaporated milk

½ tsp. vanilla extract

½ tsp. almond extract, *optional*

Nutmeg, *optional*

Cinnamon, *optional*

1. In the inner pot of the Instant Pot, melt butter using the Sauté setting. Add the rice, sugar, water, and milk, and stir.

2. Secure lid and make sure vent is at sealing. Cook on Manual on high pressure for 14 minutes. Let the pressure release naturally when cook time is up.

3. In a bowl whisk together the egg and evaporated milk.

4. Take a spoon of rice mixture and add slowly to egg mixture.

5. Return all to the inner pot and stir in the vanilla and optional almond extract.

6. Use the Sauté function and bring mixture to bubble for 30–60 seconds.

7. Stir slowly so it does not stick to the pot.

8. Use nutmeg or cinnamon to garnish if desired.

Tapioca Pudding

Nancy W. Huber, Green Park, PA

Makes 12 servings
Prep. Time: 5 minutes & Cooking Time: 15 minutes & Chilling Time: 4 hours

3 cups nonfat milk
1 cup water
1 cup small pearl tapioca
½ cup honey
4 eggs, beaten
1 tsp. vanilla extract

1. Combine the milk, water, tapioca, and honey in the inner pot of the Instant Pot.

2. Secure the lid and set the vent to sealing.

3. Manually set the cook time for 6 minutes on high pressure.

4. When the cooking time is over, let the pressure release naturally for 10 minutes, then release any remaining pressure manually.

5. When the pin drops, remove the lid. Press Cancel.

6. Press the Sauté button.

7. In a bowl, mix the eggs and vanilla. Remove about ½ cup of the pudding from the inner pot and mix vigorously with the egg/vanilla mixture to temper the eggs. Then, add this mixture back to the rest of the pudding slowly, stirring. When it comes to a boil, press Cancel and remove the inner pot from the Instant Pot.

8. Let the pudding cool down to room temperature, then chill it for at least 4 hours.

Cookies & Cream Cheesecake

Hope Comerford, Clinton Township, MI

Makes 6 servings

Prep. Time: 15 minutes & Cooking Time: 35 minutes & Chilling Time: 8 hours or overnight

Crust:

12 whole gluten-free chocolate sandwich cookies, crushed into crumbs

2 Tbsp. salted butter, melted

Cheesecake:

16 oz. cream cheese, room temperature

½ cup granulated sugar

2 large eggs, room temperature

1 Tbsp. gluten-free all-purpose flour

¼ cup heavy cream

2 tsp. pure vanilla extract

8 whole gluten-free chocolate sandwich cookies, coarsely chopped

Toppings:

1 cup whipping cream, whipped

8 whole gluten-free chocolate sandwich cookies, coarsely chopped

Chocolate sauce, *optional*

1. Tightly wrap in foil the bottom of 7-inch springform pan. Spray the inside with nonstick cooking spray.

2. In a small bowl, stir together the 12 crushed gluten-free chocolate sandwich cookies and melted butter. Press the crumbs into the bottom of the prepared pan. (I find the bottom of a glass cup is a great tool to use for this.) Place this in the freezer for 10–15 minutes.

3. In a large bowl, beat the cream cheese until smooth. (You can use an electric mixer, or stand mixer with paddle attachment.)

4. Add the sugar and mix until combined.

5. Add the eggs, one at a time, making sure each is fully incorporated before adding the next. Be sure to scrape down the bowl in between each egg.

6. Add the flour, heavy cream, and vanilla and continue to mix until smooth.

7. Gently fold in the 8 chopped gluten-free chocolate sandwich cookies and pour this batter into the pan you had in the freezer.

8. Cover the top of the pan with a piece of foil.

9. Pour 1½ cups of water into the inner pot and place the trivet in the bottom of the pot.

10. Create a "foil sling" by folding a 20-inch long piece of foil in half lengthwise two times. This "sling" will allow you to easily place and remove the springform pan from the pot.

(Continued on next page.)

11. Place the cheesecake pan in the center of the sling and carefully lower the pan into the inner pot. Fold down the excess foil from the sling to ensure the pot closes properly.

12. Lock the lid into place and make sure the vent is at sealing. Press the Manual button and cook on high pressure for 35 minutes.

13. When the Instant Pot beeps, hit the Cancel button to turn off the pressure cooker. Allow the pressure to release naturally for 10 minutes and then do a quick release to release any pressure remaining in the pot.

14. Carefully remove the lid. Gently unfold the foil sling and remove the cheesecake from the pot to a cooling rack using the foil sling "handles." Uncover the cheesecake and allow it to cool to room temperature.

15. Once the cheesecake has cooled, refrigerate it for at least 8 hours, or overnight.

16. Before serving, top with whipped cream, chopped gluten-free chocolate sandwich cookies, and a drizzle of chocolate sauce if desired.

Metric Equivalent Measurements

If you're accustomed to using metric measurements, I don't want you to be inconvenienced by the imperial measurements I use in this book.

Use this handy chart, too, to figure out the size of the slow cooker you'll need for each recipe.

Weight (Dry Ingredients)

1 oz		30 g
4 oz	¼ lb	120 g
8 oz	½ lb	240 g
12 oz	¾ lb	360 g
16 oz	1 lb	480 g
32 oz	2 lb	960 g

Slow-Cooker Sizes

1-quart	0.96 l
2-quart	1.92 l
3-quart	2.88 l
4-quart	3.84 l
5-quart	4.80 l
6-quart	5.76 l
7-quart	6.72 l
8-quart	7.68 l

Volume (Liquid Ingredients)

½ tsp.		2 ml
1 tsp.		5 ml
1 Tbsp.	½ fl oz	15 ml
2 Tbsp.	1 fl oz	30 ml
¼ cup	2 fl oz	60 ml
⅓ cup	3 fl oz	80 ml
½ cup	4 fl oz	120 ml
⅔ cup	5 fl oz	160 ml
¾ cup	6 fl oz	180 ml
1 cup	8 fl oz	240 ml
1 pt	16 fl oz	480 ml
1 qt	32 fl oz	960 ml

Length

¼ in	6 mm
½ in	13 mm
¾ in	19 mm
1 in	25 mm
6 in	15 cm
12 in	30 cm

Recipe & Ingredient Index

About the Author

Hope Comerford is a mom, wife, elementary music teacher, blogger, recipe developer, public speaker, Young Living Essential Oils essential oil enthusiast/educator, and published author. In 2013, she was diagnosed with a severe gluten intolerance, and since then has spent many hours creating easy, practical, and delicious gluten-free recipes that can be enjoyed by both those who are affected by gluten and those who are not.

Growing up, Hope spent many hours in the kitchen with her Meme (grandmother), and her love for cooking grew from there. While working on her master's degree when her daughter was young, Hope turned to her slow cookers for some salvation and sanity. It was from there she began truly experimenting with recipes and quickly learned she had the ability to get a little more creative in the kitchen and develop her own recipes.

In 2010, Hope started her blog, *A Busy Mom's Slow Cooker Adventures*, to simply share the recipes she was making with her family and friends. She never imagined people all over the world would begin visiting her page and sharing her recipes with others as well. In 2013, Hope self-published her first cookbook, *Slow Cooker Recipes 10 Ingredients or Less and Gluten-Free*, and then later wrote *The Gluten-Free Slow Cooker*.

Hope became the new brand ambassador and author of Fix-It and Forget-It in mid-2016. Since then, she has brought her excitement and creativeness to the Fix-It and Forget-It brand. Through Fix-It and Forget-It, she has written *Fix-It and Forget-It Healthy Slow Cooker Cookbook*, *Fix-It and Forget-It Healthy 5-Ingredient Cookbook*, *Fix-It and Forget-It Instant Pot Cookbook*, *Fix-It and Forget-It Plant-Based Comfort Foods Cookbook*, *Fix-It and Forget-It Diabetes Cookbook*, *Fix-It and Forget-It Instant Pot Light & Healthy Cookbook*, and many more.

Hope lives in the city of Clinton Township, Michigan, near Metro Detroit. She has been happily married to her husband and best friend, Justin, since 2008. Together they have two children, Ella and Gavin, who are her motivation, inspiration, and heart. In her spare time, Hope enjoys traveling, singing, cooking, reading books, working on wooden puzzles, spending time with friends and family, and relaxing.